Hidden Strengths

Unleashing the Crucial Leadership Skills You Already Have

Thuy Sindell and Milo Sindell

BK

Berrett–Koehler Publishers, Inc.
a BK Business book

Berrett-Koehler Publishers, Inc.
1333 Broadway, Suite 1000
Oakland, CA 94612-1921
Tel: (510) 817-2277   Fax: (510) 817-2278   www.bkconnection.com

Ordering Information
Quantity sales. Special discounts are available on quantity purchases by corporations, associations, and others. For details, contact the "Special Sales Department" at the Berrett-Koehler address above.
Individual sales. Berrett-Koehler publications are available through most bookstores. They can also be ordered directly from Berrett-Koehler: Tel: (800) 929-2929;
Fax: (802) 864-7626; www.bkconnection.com
Orders for college textbook/course adoption use. Please contact Berrett-Koehler:
Tel: (800) 929-2929; Fax: (802) 864-7626.
Orders by U.S. trade bookstores and wholesalers. Please contact Ingram Publisher Services, Tel: (800) 509-4887; Fax: (800) 838-1149; E-mail: customer.service@ingram publisherservices.com; or visit www.ingrampublisherservices.com/Ordering for details about electronic ordering.

Berrett-Koehler and the BK logo are registered trademarks of Berrett-Koehler Publishers, Inc.

Printed in the United States of America

Berrett-Koehler books are printed on long-lasting acid-free paper. When it is available, we choose paper that has been manufactured by environmentally responsible processes. These may include using trees grown in sustainable forests, incorporating recycled paper, minimizing chlorine in bleaching, or recycling the energy produced at the paper mill.

Library of Congress Cataloging-in-Publication Data

Sindell, Thuy.
    Hidden strengths : unleashing the crucial leadership skills you already have / by Thuy Sindell and Milo Sindell. —First Edition.
        pages cm
    Includes bibliographical references and index.
    ISBN 978-1-62656-283-7 (hardcover)
    1. Leadership.   I. Sindell, Milo.   II. Title.
    HD57.7.S5485 2015
    658.4'092—dc23
                                                                            2014048278

First Edition
20   19   18   17   16   15   10   9   8   7   6   5   4   3   2   1

Author photos   Abigail Huller
Cover/Jacket Designer   Brad Foltz
Cover Art   Getty Images/Aaron Foster

To Ava;

an old soul in a child's body, whose charm and wisdom enlighten us every day.

Contents

Introduction   1

PART 1 ABOUT HIDDEN STRENGTHS   5

1. What Are Hidden Strengths?   7
Why Hidden Strengths?   8
The Risk of Focusing on Weaknesses   11
The Risk of Overrelying on Strengths   14
The Reward of Focusing on Hidden Strengths   16

2. The Four Principles of Hidden Strengths   19
Principle #1: Leverage Your Traits, and Develop Your Skills   19
  Leverage Your Traits   20
  Develop Your Skills   20
Principle #2: The Middle Is the Source for Development   21
Principle #3: Practice, Practice, Practice   23
Principle #4: Always Be Working on Your Hidden Strengths   24

PART 2 UNCOVERING THE GOLD MINE OF OPPORTUNITY   27

3. Identifying Your Natural Strengths, Hidden Strengths, and Weaknesses   29
The Twenty-Eight Skills   30
  Leading Self   32
  Leading Others   34
  Leading the Organization   36
  Leading Implementation   38

4. Reviewing Your Results   41
   Your Hidden Strengths Report   43

PART 3 HARNESSING YOUR POTENTIAL   45

5. Making Your Hidden Strengths Work for You   47
   Hidden Strengths Development Plan   47
      Step 1: Find Your Motivation   47
      Step 2: Identify Your Goals   49
      Step 3: Choose Your Hidden Strengths to Develop   50
      Step 4: Turn Your Hidden Strengths into Learned Strengths   59
      Step 5: Evaluate Your Progress   60

6. Leading Your Evolution   62
   Sustainability   62
   The Never-Ending Adventure   63
   Share the Love   63

   Appendix A: The Twenty-Eight Skills and Why They Matter   65
   Appendix B: Hidden Strengths Development Worksheet   77
   Notes   79
   Accessing Your Free Hidden Strengths Profile   81
   Acknowledgements   83
   Index   85
   About the Authors   87

Introduction

A ll of us would like to know the secret of great leadership. Well, here's the secret: It depends. It depends on what you are naturally good at, what you are terrible at, and what you decide to develop— those Hidden Skills that are in the middle.

My name is Thuy (pronounced TWEE) Sindell. I've been an executive coach since the late 1990s, and I am also the president of Skyline Group's Coaching Division. I've worked with hundreds of business leaders over the years, and this is my opportunity to share with you the patterns and themes I've observed and the ways I've supported leaders in their growth. I have a no-nonsense style, so you can expect the information in this book to be direct and to get you quickly on your leadership path.

My name is Milo Sindell. Thuy and I work together, have written four books together, *and* we are happily married. I head Skyline Group's C4X Division, which is our hybrid technology coaching solution, as well as drive the direction and market position of Skyline. I have a passion for helping leaders make an impact on the world. I wrote this book to provide a proven methodology for lifelong learning and professional development to both current and emerging leaders.

We have worked with many companies—from hi-tech companies to insurance companies and everything in between. We have helped employees to increase their effectiveness in various departments and in positions like engineering and sales. Across professions and industries, we have noted certain patterns in human behavior and,

1

more important, consistent processes for identifying and developing the right skills at the right time to get you to your next level. We are talking, of course, about your Hidden Strengths.

Research has shown that effective leaders evolve and grow throughout their careers, whereas failed leaders get stuck in a pattern of overusing their strengths to the point of staleness.[1] Our emphasis on the relationship between constant learning, increasing agility, and long-term leadership success is not new. What is new is our system for creating a growth mind-set, identifying learning opportunities, and setting the stage for your ongoing professional evolution as an aspiring or current leader.

Many leaders and aspiring leaders usually concentrate on trying to leverage their Natural Strengths (the top 20 percent of skills) or minimize their Weaknesses (the bottom 10 percent). Our tendency as humans is to focus on the extremes. We distill things down to what we don't do well and try to fix them, or we rely on what comes easily and lean on our strengths.

Let's use Barbara, a woman we worked with a few years ago, as an example. Barbara believed that if she could only "fix" her weakness of being a poor presenter, she would be a great leader. Great leadership, however, depends on who you are, your environment, and what you are being called upon to achieve. There is no one weakness you need to fix to get there or one formula that works for everyone. Personalized learning is the key. That's why executive coaching is such a fast-growing solution to developing leaders.

What we have found in our executive coaching experience is that the most fertile ground for leadership and professional growth is the 70 percent of skills that fall in the middle of your range. These are your Hidden Strengths; you are not great at them (yet), but you're certainly not failing in those areas either. This is where your Hidden Strengths are hiding out, waiting to be unleashed.

We want to raise people's awareness of their Hidden Strengths. Everyone has them, and everyone can develop them! We know from experience that constantly identifying and developing your Hidden

Strengths are the keys to career and leadership development in today's evolving work environment. In this book, we share this highly effective results-oriented approach to leadership.

Imagine if you stayed locked in the belief that what worked well yesterday will work well today—and tomorrow and the day after that. You would eventually figure out that doing what you always do leads to professional stagnation. Alternately, the Hidden Strengths methodology shows you how to tap into and transform underdeveloped skills for ongoing professional development throughout your career.

The first part of this book introduces the concept of Hidden Strengths and explores the immense potential of this middle range of skills as a source for continued growth. The second part is a guide to assessing and getting familiar with your Hidden Strengths, your Natural Strengths, and your Weaknesses. The final part is a road map for determining which of your Hidden Strengths best supports your goals.

One last thing: *Hidden Strengths* is a book for leaders and aspiring leaders—basically, anybody who is motivated to learn more about themselves and how they can grow in their careers. We see leadership as a mentality. It involves being proactive about how you present yourself to the world whether you're an individual contributor, a middle-level manager, or a CEO.

When leadership is a state of mind, you prime yourself to grow and succeed, no matter your level or position. In other words, leadership development is professional development. And at each stage of your career, identifying and developing your Hidden Strengths are the means to unleashing the crucial leadership skills you already have. There's a gold mine of opportunity in the middle!

About Hidden Strengths

Part 1 provides an overview of the Hidden Strengths methodology and why we believe it is a powerful way to optimize your continued leadership development. We explore the assumptions around the development of skills and set the groundwork for how you can transform Hidden Strengths into Learned Strengths at the top of your skill set.

1

What Are Hidden Strengths?

When we are faced with a new challenge—playing a new game, building a new relationship, or getting a promotion—we usually rely on what we consider our strengths. And why not? Shouldn't what has worked for us in the past work in the future?

On the other end of the skill spectrum, however, we tend to get mired in futile attempts to fix things and improve the skills that are our true weaknesses. Our glaring shortcomings become the most obvious targets for improvement. Why is it so easy to focus on the extremes—our strengths and weaknesses—and overlook the gold that lies in the middle? This book is about what lies between what you are already great at and what you are inherently just not good at doing: your Hidden Strengths. These underdeveloped skills are your richest resources for growth.

In our experience working with hundreds of leaders, we have identified twenty-eight skills that are necessary to achieve professional success (see Chapter 3). What we have also found is that for each person, these twenty-eight skills fall into three buckets: Natural Strengths, Weaknesses, and Hidden Strengths (Figure 1).

1. Natural Strengths (the top 20 percent): the abilities you default to because they come easily
2. Weaknesses (the bottom 10 percent): the things you are simply not good at and will probably never be good at
3. Hidden Strengths (the middle 70 percent): the things you neither excel nor fail at

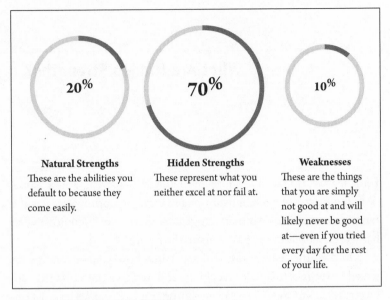

Figure 1. The Three Buckets of Skills

Despite being the largest pool, the skills in the middle are often overlooked by people who are too busy relying on their strengths or working on improving their weaknesses; that's why we call them "hidden." Effective leaders evolve and grow throughout their careers, whereas failed leaders get stuck in a pattern of overusing their strengths.[2] It is important to call out that our emphasis on the relationship between continual growth and long-term leadership success is not new. What is new is our system for creating a growth mind-set, identifying learning opportunities, and setting the stage for your ongoing professional evolution.

Why Hidden Strengths?

The subject of strengths in both popular and business culture has been a positive force helping raise the bar on personal and professional development. In *Now, Discover Your Strengths*, the book that ostensibly started the strengths movement, Marcus Buckingham and Donald Clifton[3] define a *strength* as a combination of the following:

1. Your talents (natural traits or propensities)
2. The knowledge required (both content/classroom-related and experiential)
3. The skills (or steps) you need to actually do it

When these three components—talents, knowledge, and skills—come together naturally, we call it a Natural Strength (Figure 2). What is the likelihood of this occurring? The answer is about 20 percent—as in your top 20 percent of skills.

Understanding what you are naturally good at is very valuable in finding the right job or career path. The more overlap there is between what you are required to do and what you are inherently good at, the easier your life will be. Conversely, finding yourself in situations where you are forced to rely on your Weaknesses—meaning areas

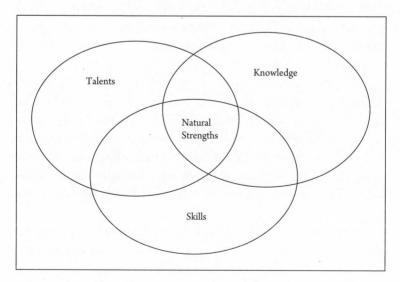

Figure 2. Natural Strengths

where you have no talents, knowledge, or skills—will make it much more difficult to be successful in your chosen profession. From a job security and personal well-being standpoint, you should not be in a role that requires you to rely heavily on your Weaknesses.

Understanding your Natural Strengths and Weaknesses is most relevant for determining job fit. Awareness of these two extremes sets the parameters that allow you to find your place in the work world. Where Hidden Strengths come into play is in the ongoing evolution of your career. For the vast majority of us, the skills we are hired for or are naturally good at in a given role will not be the skills we will need to progress. So how do we remain agile and ensure continued professional development? The answer here is by developing the rich pool of Hidden Strengths in our middle 70 percent.

Developing Hidden Strengths is fairly straightforward. Anybody can do it! First, it requires identifying which of your skills fall in the middle 70 percent range. You can find the Hidden Strengths Self-Assessment to help you with this first step at HiddenStrengths.com. Second, you must identify which of your Hidden Strengths you want to focus on (there will be many to choose from!), depending on your professional goals. Third, with practice and focus, you can begin to develop those Hidden Strengths and move them from the middle 70 percent to the top of your skill set.

Take this example: Jenny is an individual contributor in the Finance Department. She has a natural talent for *Influencing Others*, but she has never had the opportunity to use it. To unleash this Hidden Strength, she needs the knowledge and skills to reveal it. But what if her boss never gives her the opportunity to lead? Because she is not familiar with the existence of this Hidden Strength, she may never ask for leadership responsibility. Resulting in a lost opportunity to grow into a leadership role.

Here's another case to consider: Reese, a middle manager in a paper factory, is intent on moving up the career ladder. At the moment, his Natural Strengths seem to be well aligned with his job, but he is ambitiously focused on what comes next. He takes the Hidden Strengths assessment and discovers that *Influencing Others* is one of his Hidden Strengths. He sees how this skill would be helpful if he were to be promoted to regional manager, so he takes the time to learn about it and practices developing it. Unfortunately, influencing others doesn't come naturally to him—it's not a talent—but with time and experience, he develops the knowledge and skills to be quite influential. *Influencing Others* becomes a Learned Strength for him, and by practicing on the job, he has proven to his boss that he's ready for more leadership responsibility.

Unlike Natural Strengths, identifying and transforming your Hidden Strengths into Learned Strengths are actions you control and drive. You decide how to evolve, grow, and change to meet the demands of the world around you. We look at this as not only empowering but exciting! Even if the stars don't align and endow you with all the right Natural Strengths, you can still become a leader and top performer in your chosen field. The first critical step is an awareness of your Hidden Strengths.

The Risk of Focusing on Weaknesses

The problem with focusing on weaknesses is that it takes a tremendous amount of effort to move the needle to a point where you can demonstrate improvement. Using economic terms, the investment in resources (i.e., time, dollars, and energy) and opportunity costs (i.e., not focusing on other skill development opportunities that yield higher returns quicker), result in a negative return. We suggest a bandage approach for managing your Weaknesses: avoid or delegate them if you can, or learn to do them adequately if you must, knowing full well you might never be great at it.

In situations where you have to perform despite a weakness, you should invest the necessary time and energy to become proficient, but you shouldn't try to turn your weaknesses into strengths. For example, if you are a CEO of a publicly traded company and you are horrible at giving presentations, you don't have the luxury of delegating this kind of responsibility. In this case, you will have to learn to speak publicly with a minimum level of competence.

You should invest the necessary time and energy to become proficient, but you shouldn't try to turn your weaknesses into strengths. In some cases, this will never happen, so just accept it and move on. Spend only as much time and effort on it as you need to so you can focus on other, more fruitful endeavors.

One of our clients, Nicolas, was a great organizer and manager of very complex projects and problems. He knew where to get the right people and resources and how to organize them to get the job done. *Planning and Organizing* and *Leading Implementation* were the Natural Strengths that he consistently depended on. Nicolas was tasked with building a world-class team. His manager wanted the most experienced industry leaders in product management to *want* to work for him. The problem was that people perceived Nicolas as an execution machine who lacked vision and was too focused on results. He often alienated others along the way.

The challenge for Nicolas was to evolve from a leader who was known for getting things done whether or not his team felt good about it to a leader who was more inclusive. He also needed to be more of a product visionary and to communicate his strategic thinking more effectively.

Nicolas's lowest score was on *Inspirational Vision*; he couldn't see more than two years out. He also lacked technical expertise because he was not an engineer, and he didn't have the strong connection to the industry that his manager and peers did. He would need to spend a lot of time and energy honing his technical skills and building a stronger network of thought leaders to get marginally better at these skills. It didn't make any sense to focus on them. We encouraged Nicolas to let go of trying to develop his weakest skills and instead work on three of his Hidden Strengths that could be more rapidly learned and applied: *Leading Others, Verbal Communication,* and *Strategic Thinking.*

Within a few weeks of focusing on *Leading Others,* Nicolas strengthened his ability to recruit top-notch people. At first, Nicolas did not want to hire people whom he perceived as more talented or skilled than he was; he was afraid it would highlight his own short-comings. Once he got over that fear, however, he was able to make much more effective hiring decisions. Nicolas took the time to thoroughly screen prospective new hires. He carefully onboarded and integrated them to ensure they became productive quickly. He developed processes to help them hone their skills to fit the needs of the organization. Finally, he provided ongoing feedback, mentoring, and coaching. Over time, with his help, these employees became valuable contributors to the company.

Nicolas also focused on growing and leveraging his *Strategic Thinking* and *Verbal Communication* to counterbalance his lack of *Inspirational Vision*. He learned how to reframe his projects and decisions as if they were a chess game. If he thought of the end goal one year from now as the equivalent of check and checkmate, he could identify the moves he needed to make now and in the future with an eye to the resources he had at hand. His deployment of these Hidden Strengths along with his Natural Strength of *Planning and Organizing* made it possible for Nicolas to give his team and coworkers the opportunity to be involved, feel included, and understand his procedures.

We have also worked with many great leaders who were the opposite of Nicolas. They were excellent at getting people fired up and excited about their visions. They naturally defaulted to rallying employees around what was possible. However, they were horrible at presenting details, planning, and organizing the work that needed to be done to realize the vision. They rightly ignored developing their weaknesses and instead delegated the planning and details to the managers who reported to them (who were much more analytical) and to their assistants (who were much more organized). To better bridge the gap between *Inspirational Vision* and *Effectiveness*, they built their Hidden Strengths of *Teamwork and Collaboration* and *Partnering and Relationship Building*, focusing their time and attention on developing the strategic relationships that were necessary to get the job done.

The Risk of Overrelying on Strengths

The problem with relying on our Natural Strengths is that it can lead to *stagnation*. We all unconsciously default to the skills that come easily to us, but always relying on a particular set of skills—even if you're great at them—is not enough to stay on top. It is a potential dead end. Your agility in evolving your abilities to meet an ever-changing environment will be the hallmark and foundation of your success.

If agility leads to success in today's business environment, then rigidity and overreliance on current strengths must be avoided at all costs. It would be so much easier if we could just stick with what we do well today for the rest of our lives. But research shows us that to be effective, leaders must constantly adapt to their changing environments. Those who don't adapt eventually see their strengths turn into weaknesses through overuse.[4] In fact, leaders who lack the insight, ability, and willingness to evolve will find that their environment provides the most damning feedback in the form of career stagnation or ejection from their roles.

James was one of our executive coaching clients. He wasn't great at listening, but he wasn't terrible at it either. He found that focusing on this skill set was a waste of his time because he knew exactly what it meant to display *Listening* skills, such as making eye contact, checking for understanding, and paraphrasing for clarity. We pointed out to him that although he knew the skills, he didn't demonstrate them most of the time. He only did it when the stakes were high or when there was a senior leader in the room, but not with his peers and direct reports.

James's story is an example of how we often "pooh-pooh" the obvious things that hold us back from being even more amazing: our Hidden Strengths. He was faced with the decision to develop his *Listening* skills or risk not getting promoted because people didn't like to work with him. Unfortunately, however, this knowledge failed to translate into behavior, and it continued to undermine his effectiveness with his peers. Why would James sabotage his career instead of developing a skill he could easily turn into a Learned Strength?

Consider another example: Bill was a manager in a large manufacturing company. His work often involved managing complex projects, and he became adept at assembling and leading teams. His *Assertiveness* and technical know-how were his strongest leadership attributes. At his level in the organization, he was considered trustworthy. Not surprisingly, senior management swiftly spotted his talent. He was moved to headquarters for a job rotation that would be good preparation for further career advancement.

Unfortunately, things started to unravel when Bill was at headquarters. Naturally, he relied on his current strengths, but the head office was political, and Bill soon found that his straight talk hit many wrong notes. He received feedback that he didn't seem to fully understand the nuances and complexities of situations and was encouraged to develop better skills for *Organizational Awareness.* Bill tried to curb his directness, but he was never able to adopt his superiors' politically savvy behaviors. He struggled with his values and never came around to accepting that the politics were what they were. Instead, he shunned them with his forthrightness in public forums.

Bill stayed with the company, but he never advanced in his position. His rigidity prevented him from navigating the politics. He resisted growing his Hidden Strength of *Organizational Awareness.* Although he was good at being direct and making sound technical decisions, he needed to find the time and place when people were more apt to listen. In addition, he had to be mindful of the organizational history of the company and learn how to help others save face. The development of strong *Organizational Awareness* skills would have made Bill more trustworthy at both senior *and* lower levels of the organization. With that trust, he may have had the opportunity to influence the organization and even shift the politics, but he couldn't embrace adapting his behavior to work within the system.

You have probably met more than one failed leader like Bill in your organization. His story illustrates perfectly how difficult it is for leaders to find a balance between the skills that got them to a certain level and the agility necessary to learn new skills. It is risky to assume that the professional skills that got you where you are today will keep you going for the rest of your career. The consequences of stagnation are all around you. Golf courses around the world are full of un-evolved leaders who were invited to leave the world of industry.

The Reward of Focusing on Hidden Strengths

As you are probably figuring out by now, the rewards of focusing on Hidden Strengths are continued professional development and career advancement. Knowing your Hidden Strengths is the key to identifying and growing the right skills at the right time for success.

Most leaders start their careers as strong individual contributors who demonstrate proficiency in their area of expertise and are rewarded with more responsibility—namely, management. In most companies, saying "no" to increased responsibility is a career killer, so despite little experience, interest, or demonstrated skills in managing others, strong individual contributors find themselves in positions of leadership. For the most part, these new leaders are able to learn on the fly, use traits they are naturally good at, and effectively survive each successive promotion. But the problem with this model is that sooner or later, even the most adaptable, highly skilled technical leaders reach a point where they can no longer rely solely on their Natural Strengths. Long-term success as a leader requires the ability to learn, adapt, and grow with each new challenge brought on by new promotions, projects, and demands.[5]

Whether or not you choose a formal leadership path, to be successful, you must use different skill sets at different stages of your career. This is an absolute certainty. No matter what your job is, the world around you is dynamic. New challenges will emerge, and adaptation requires developing new skills and drawing from new perspectives. Optimizing the right Hidden Strengths at the right time is what leads to ongoing growth. In our experience, the very foundation of professional and leadership development is constantly identifying and developing Hidden Strengths. That is what led to Alice's success. Here is her story.

Alice is the founder and CEO of a start-up that has just been recognized as one of the most innovative companies in the country. Throughout her career from software engineer to entrepreneur and CEO, her focus has been on achieving her goals, while at the same time paying attention to those around her.

Early in her career as an engineer, she observed the leaders in her organization, examining their career paths and leadership qualities. She compared them to the employees who remained individual contributors and saw that the most successful individual contributors were the ones who honed their skills. They were naturally good at what they did, and their aspirations centered on becoming the best they could be in their chosen field. Conversely, those who successfully moved into leadership positions embraced the need to adopt a range of skills beyond their technical competencies. They learned to adapt to changing situations as greater responsibilities presented themselves and as new operational challenges emerged.

Alice regularly sought feedback and opportunities from mentors and leaders she respected to determine new skills that needed to be developed. Her evolution from software engineer with the technical skills of problem solving and being detail oriented began with developing a broader range of hidden leadership strengths like *Flexibility* and *Entrepreneurship*. Alice credits her success as a leader to her ability to challenge herself and transform these Hidden Strengths into Learned Strengths.

There is no doubt that our world is getting more complex and interconnected. Everything is evolving to be bigger and faster and to include greater interdependencies. This shift is not likely to slow down. Your ability to adapt to an ever-changing environment is critical. More than anything else, you must be agile.

The modern workplace is one where your ideals and aspirations for the perfect job, perfect fit, perfect boss, and perfect culture collide with the real challenges of poor leadership, tight resources, compressed deadlines, and the need for you to stretch your professional abilities every day. Identifying and developing your Hidden Strengths involve a realistic you-driven approach to meeting those challenges. Success requires proactively developing the necessary knowledge and skills to achieve your goals, taking control of your career, and showing the world you have what it takes to evolve and thrive in today's workplace.

2

The Four Principles of Hidden Strengths

The rocket fuel for your development resides in your middle. With awareness, effort, and the appropriate resources, you can quickly turn Hidden Strengths into Learned Strengths. They may never come as easily to you as your Natural Strengths, but they will be equally as valuable to you and your organization.

The Hidden Strengths methodology, composed of four principles, provides an important framework for unleashing your Hidden Strengths and ensuring your ongoing professional development:

1. Leverage your traits, and develop your skills.
2. The middle is the source for your development.
3. Practice, practice, practice.
4. Always be working on your Hidden Strengths.

Principle #1: Leverage Your Traits, and Develop Your Skills

Being effective in the workplace requires a combination of underlying traits and skills. You are born with certain traits or talents, and they are not particularly malleable. On the other hand, skills are an adaptation to your environment. For example, if you are naturally opinionated and outspoken and grow up in an Asian culture, you learn to be quiet even though you feel the compulsion to speak. Learning to keep your mouth shut when you are naturally outspoken is a skill. The workplace often poses challenges where traits may need to be tempered or leveraged and new skills developed as a response to your organization's needs.

Leverage Your Traits

Your traits act as a foundation for what you do and how you do it. For instance, great subject matter expertise in finance will only get you so far if you have the social traits of an irate three-year-old. Conversely, great subject matter expertise combined with Yoda-like insight on how to woo your audience will clear your path to the corner office.

Common leadership traits include competitiveness, adaptability, focus, inclusiveness, and self-assurance. Awareness of the traits you possess and how they interact is another important component of effective leadership. As a reminder, we see leadership not as a formal position or career path but as a mind-set that is focused on growth and self-improvement. As such, leadership can occur at all levels and regardless of title. The most important factors are an awareness of how you present yourself to the world and being proactive about your development. As a leader or aspiring leader, you must continuously call upon *all* of your traits. Of course, in certain circumstances, different traits will need to be leveraged.

Develop Your Skills

Unlike traits, skills can be developed, morphed, or even transformed. Utilizing your Hidden Strengths is about ensuring you are proactively developing the needed skills in your role, regardless of whether or not you have the natural traits. You should be constantly reflecting on the skills you want to develop. Realistically, however, skill development is most often brought on by circumstance. Rarely does an internal alarm clock go off, jolting you to hone your influencing skills or to work more effectively cross-functionally. The Hidden Strengths framework challenges you to move beyond this stimulus-response dynamic by consistently reflecting on your current skills in relation to current or future demands.

The story of former Xerox CEO, Anne Mulcahy, emphasizes the importance of leveraging situationally relevant traits while developing the necessary leadership skills on the job. In 2001, to the surprise of many, Mulcahy was named CEO of Xerox Corporation. During her twenty-four years at Xerox, she never planned on becoming CEO. Now she was tasked with turning the company around after a steady period of underperformance. "I certainly hadn't been groomed to become a CEO," Mulcahy said. "I didn't have a very sophisticated financial background, and I had to make up for my lack of formal training. I had to make up for it with intense on-the-job learning."[6] At the time, the company was on the brink of bankruptcy with over $17 billion of debt and six years of financial losses. It was also in the middle of a Securities and Exchange Commission investigation. With Mulcahy at the helm, Xerox's debt fell from ten times its equity to less than two times in four years.

Mulcahy effectively leveraged her focused, competitive, and achievement-oriented nature as she developed skills like effective communication, financial acumen, and tough decision making. The necessity of learning on-the-job forced her to quickly evolve her skill set to meet the challenges in her midst.

Mulcahy developed new skills, such as making hard financial decisions and organizing trade-offs. Although she had some financial understanding, she had to learn a lot more. She was used to making tough decisions, but now she had to do it on a much larger and more visible scale. She leveraged her traits to help her develop new skills or—using our terminology—to turn her Hidden Strengths into Learned Strengths.

Principle #2: The Middle Is the Source for Development

In 2000, the Sales Executive Council studied 625 sales representatives across eleven different organizations. The median sale value was $4.5 million. When they took the high performers (i.e., the top

20 percent) and calculated their sales, it came out to $158 million across the eleven companies. They calculated that 5 percent more sales from the top 20 percent would yield an additional $7.9 million.

The Sales Executive Council also looked at the middle performers (the middle 60 percent) that produced $271 million. Getting 5 percent more out of them would yield another $13.5 million—almost double what you would get out of the high performers! Although the top salespeople achieved much higher sales individually, it didn't make sense to squeeze another 5 percent out of them versus 5 percent out of each of the middle performers. This study is a perfect example of how the middle is where the real potential for development lies.

Just like middle performers, the Hidden Strengths in the middle of your skill spectrum represent the largest pool for development, as well as the most room for growth. How much better will you get at your Natural Strengths when they are already your default? How far will you push the needle on your Weaknesses before you miss out on a more fruitful opportunity? In contrast, you possess numerous Hidden Strengths that will make a significant difference in your abilities as a leader and how you are perceived without risking stagnation or requiring as big an investment as your Weaknesses will.

Jennifer, one of our clients, was promoted to manager for being a strong engineer. Over the years she continued to climb the ranks with ease but seemed to hit a wall with respect to certain soft skills. Specifically, she was not inspirational or bold enough with her ideas.

The organization wanted Jennifer to keep growing, so they hired us to coach her. We did a 360-degree assessment, which included feedback from her manager, peers, direct reports, cross-functional partners, and internal customers and revealed her Hidden Strengths of *Creativity and Innovation* and *Influencing Others*. With help, Jennifer could learn to push for new ways of doing things and how to convey her ideas with more passion and excitement.

The 360-degree assessment also revealed some definite Weaknesses: Jennifer was pretty bad at building relationships. She was so introverted that she didn't see any value in spending time with people socially or after work, and no amount of coaching could change this aspect of her personality. Helping Jennifer learn how to be more sociable would have been a painful experience for her and those around her because of her shyness. Instead, using the bandage approach, we worked with Jennifer on becoming more competent at the mandatory one-on-one meetings she had with her team, but we didn't waste time trying to encourage her to socialize with others outside the workplace.

Most of our work with Jennifer focused on helping her passionately articulate the ideas she already had in her head, making them more inspiring in terms of the messaging, and finding the best ways in which to share them to influence others and get them onboard. What opportunities could she take advantage of to make her ideas even better? What framework could she use for putting her ideas into words? What word choices could she make to convey passion? How could she use her body language and tone of voice to demonstrate excitement?

When Jennifer was able to focus on taking something she already had and making it better, she quickly saw the return on her investment. Having her ideas heard made her much more excited about work, and her ability to demonstrate the value in her thinking made her a leader in the company.

Principle #3: Practice, Practice, Practice

The Hidden Strengths framework provides space to excel because you can't naturally be great at everything you take on or is directed your way. To become good at something, you need to put in the time and effort. Many studies show that deliberate practice is closely related to the attained level of performance of many types of experts, such as musicians, chess players, and athletes.[7] The same goes for leadership skills. Consistent focus and practice are what transform Hidden Strengths into Learned Strengths.

When confronted with things we aren't particularly good at, most of us will avoid them, so moving a skill from the middle 70 percent to the top 20 percent is a legitimate achievement that instills a great sense of pride. Take the story of the CEO who did not naturally exude *Self-Confidence*. It wasn't a Weakness, because he did believe in his own abilities. He just needed practice getting out of his head, being more assertive, and clearly expressing his opinions and visions. By the time he was in his fourth year as CEO, he had gotten pretty good at presenting himself in a self-assured manner. Those who worked with him knew it took a lot of focus for him to portray that persona, but it worked, and he was darn proud of himself.

Before we go on, think about what gives your success meaning. More than likely, the sweetness of success is related to the effort required and the challenge that was overcome. Think back to the last thing you achieved that was significant. How did you do it, and what obstacles, challenges, or learning was required? Your success would be empty or even trivial without the effort made to overcome the challenges you faced. The storyteller in all of us wants to be able to tell a story of victory over a challenge. Without challenge or adversity, there is no compelling story. Putting in the work to transform Hidden Strengths into Learned Strengths pushes us, reinforces our convictions, and gives meaning to our victories. This is how we grow.

Principle #4: Always Be Working on Your Hidden Strengths

Your leadership story should be one of striving for new heights and staying ahead of the curve. Whenever someone asks you what you are up to, you want to be able to answer them with something meaningful, like developing a new skill or two. That is why we suggest that you always be working on one to three Hidden Strengths at any given time.

Continuously developing your Hidden Strengths also helps you to stretch your brainpower. Research has demonstrated that pushing yourself to develop new skills stimulates new neural pathways, causing new brain circuitry to be developed that allows for more complex and adaptive thinking.[8] In a 2009 *New York Times* article on training the brain, Kathleen Taylor, a professor in the Doctorate in Educational Leadership Program at Saint Mary's College of California, explained, "The brain is plastic and continues to change, not in getting bigger but allowing for greater complexity and deeper understanding."[9] According to Taylor, adult learners should not only focus on learning new facts but also on expanding their perspectives and openly confronting thoughts that are contrary to their own. To us this includes examining your default tendencies and identifying alternative behaviors or Hidden Strengths that may not come as easily. "There's a place for information," Taylor said. "We need to know stuff. But we need to move beyond that and challenge our perception of the world. . . . We have to crack the cognitive egg and scramble it up. And if you learn something this way, when you think of it again, you'll have an overlay of complexity you didn't have before."

In the same article, the late Jack Mezirow, at the time an emeritus professor of Adult and Continuing Education at Teachers College at Columbia University, proposed that adults learn best if presented with what he calls a "disorienting dilemma," or something that "helps you critically reflect on the assumptions you've acquired."[10] "As adults, we have all those brain pathways built up, and we need to look at our insights critically," he said. "This is the best way for adults to learn. And if we do it, we can remain sharp."

The road to success is paved with ongoing reflection and skill development. This means you need to be constantly observing your environment for current and upcoming trends, changes, and shifts and identifying the skills you want to develop next. This focus ensures that you are constantly learning and evolving as a leader and, as Mezirow put it, that you keep your most important professional resource (your brain) sharp.

Uncovering the Gold Mine of Opportunity

Part 2 discusses how you can identify your Hidden Strengths using the Hidden Strengths Assessment (HiddenStrengths.com). It also introduces the twenty-eight skills you will be assessed on and the four categories they fall into: Leading Self, Leading Others, Leading the Organization, and Leading Implementation. Finally, it provides insight into how to interpret your results through the lens of your continued leadership and career growth.

3

Identifying Your Natural Strengths, Hidden Strengths, and Weaknesses

The most valuable information you can have is an understanding of your current abilities. With a clear view of your Natural Strengths, Weaknesses, and, especially, Hidden Strengths, you can identify where to focus your attention to help you move to the next level of your profession.

As we discussed in Chapters 1 and 2, pushing your growth and moving outside of your comfort zone are the keys to your personal and professional evolution. More often than not, it takes an event—in this case, getting critical data about where you stand—to jump-start the growth process. Gathering this information is easy to do and should be done annually to keep you on top of your game.

Several methods are available for assessing your skills, including self-assessments and 360-degree assessments. The latter tend to be more robust because they incorporate feedback from all of your stakeholders, including your managers, peers, direct reports, cross-functional partners, and customers (internal or external). In a 360-degree assessment, you might find that comments from various groups differ. For example, your peers and your manager may be harder on you than your team is. You might also find there are gaps between how you see yourself and how others perceive you. (In our experience, this is usually the case.) All of this information is valuable to your professional development.

The two types of 360-degree assessments are informational interviews and online 360s with quantitative and qualitative data. Although informational interviews are richer in data, fewer people can participate because they are conducted either in person or over the phone, take a lot of time, and generate a lot of qualitative data. Conversely, online 360s enable more people to participate, and because at least some of the data are quantitative, they can be grouped and analyzed in many ways (e.g., by audience or by percentiles relative to the population) to provide more insights.

For ease of use and obtaining results, the *Hidden Strengths Assessment* is available as a free online self-assessment. To get the most out of this book, we encourage you to take the online version at HiddenStrengths.com. In addition to a personalized *Hidden Strengths Report*, you will receive a guide to help you create a customized skill development plan based on your goals.

The Twenty-Eight Skills

In our work with thousands of leaders in small and large companies from a cross section of industries, we have identified four categories of skills critical to professional success:

1. Leading Self: How aware are you of your skills and limitations? How strong is your ability to self-regulate?
2. Leading Others: How do you interact with others in the organization?
3. Leading the Organization: To what extent do you think about the direction of the organization and how you function within it?
4. Leading Implementation: How are you ensuring that things get done?

Within each of these four categories are seven specific skills, for a total of twenty-eight skills (Table 1). The Hidden Strengths Assessment is an evaluation on the basis of these twenty-eight skills. Understanding the strength of your skills relative to each of the four categories will help you to identify your next opportunities for professional development. The following sections describe the twenty-eight skills

Table 1 The Twenty-Eight Skills

Category	Skill
Leading Self	
	Emotional Control
	Flexibility
	Integrity
	Resilience
	Self-Confidence
	Executive Presence
	Work/Life Balance
Leading Others	
	Assertiveness
	Conflict Resolution
	Influencing Others
	Listening
	Partnering and Relationship Building
	Teamwork and Collaboration
	Verbal Communication
Leading the Organization	
	Creativity and Innovation
	Entrepreneurship
	External Awareness
	Inspirational Vision
	Organizational Awareness
	Service Motivation
	Strategic Thinking
Leading Implementation	
	Coaching and Mentoring
	Customer Focus
	Delegation
	Effectiveness
	Monitoring Performance
	Planning and Organizing
	Thoroughness

and explain why they matter. Go ahead and familiarize yourself with them before you take the assessment. For a deeper exploration of these skills and why they matter, please see Appendix A on page 65.

Leading Self

This category of skills is about how you regulate the kind of person you want to be as a leader and a professional. When you are grounded in who you are and can manage your emotions, you exude a quiet confidence that inspires others. These skills may appear more like natural talents or traits, but they in fact can be learned. We have worked with thousands of leaders to help them build stronger skills in these areas, and you can do it, too!

Emotional Control. This is your ability to maintain a professional, respectful attitude during stressful situations. It is the opposite of being reactive and allowing your emotions to get the best of you. When you operate at a high level of *Emotional Control*, you are able to prevent knee-jerk reactions that can damage relationships and your reputation. The more *Emotional Control* you demonstrate, the more approachable and credible you seem, and the more people will be willing to follow your lead. Others trust that no matter what happens, you can keep your cool and handle any situation that comes at you.

Flexibility. This is your ability to bend without breaking. You are open to change and new information. You adapt quickly in response to shifting conditions and willingly compromise instead of rigidly sticking to your ideas. When you are flexible, you don't feel stuck if something doesn't work out or when changes are needed; instead, you look at possible alternatives and choose the best one. The more *Flexibility* you demonstrate, the more likely you are to remain relevant and contribute in a meaningful way.

Integrity. This is your ability to do the right thing. You demonstrate the highest standards of ethics and fairness. You operate in a state of alignment between your beliefs, values, and actions. *Integrity* inspires trust and confidence because people perceive you as incorruptible. They believe you have their best interests and the best interests of the organization at heart. The more *Integrity* you demonstrate, the more others will be motivated to buy into your ideas and follow your lead.

Resilience. This is your ability to deal with stressful circumstances and still perform effectively. You have the mental, emotional, and physical stamina to withstand adversity. You demonstrate focus and optimism under pressure, and you can be trusted to turn disruptions into growth opportunities. When you operate with *Resilience,* the uncertainties inherent in today's business conditions, including reorganizations, downsizings, mergers, and budget constraints, do not throw you off. By remaining productive and levelheaded amid the chaos, you show that you can take on higher levels of responsibility.

Self-Confidence. This is your ability to express your belief in your own capabilities without arrogance. You know you have what it takes to get the job done. There is clarity and directness in the opinions you express and the actions you take. When you operate with *Self-Confidence,* you exert powerful influence over others. They believe in your abilities because they can see that you believe in yourself.

Executive Presence. This is your ability to command the room. You display poise, authenticity, competence, and commitment. People respect you and want you in the driver's seat. When you exercise *Executive Presence,* you deliver messages in a way that inspires others to action. They want to follow your lead. In fact, *Executive Presence* is the essence of leadership. It is earned authority. It is how you influence others and the direction of your team, department, or organization. It is one of the most vital business skills you can develop and master.

Work/Life Balance. This is your ability to achieve balance between the professional and personal aspects of your life. You feel fully engaged in both of these important areas and can easily switch focus from one to the other. Although balance is typically considered a 50:50 ratio, *Work/Life Balance* is more subjective. The ratios differ for different people and for different times in their lives. With *Work/Life Balance* you avoid frustrations from your work spilling over into your personal life, and vice versa. It is key to a healthy lifestyle and a sustainable and fulfilling livelihood.

Leading Others

This category of skills is about how you relate to others and form strong working relationships. We find that this area can be particularly hard for people who are more results oriented and focused on the end product. The thing to remember is that almost all projects are a team effort and results cannot be achieved by one person alone. Relating well to people and managing their expectations and needs are essential parts of the process that cannot be overlooked.

Assertiveness. This is your ability to confidently express an opinion without injecting a negative emotional component. You present your views and make requests in a direct, open manner. Additionally, you don't back down when opposing views are presented. Instead, you have an open exchange of ideas to try to find a solution that works for all. When you exercise *Assertiveness*, you get your point across to others clearly without leaving a bad taste in their mouths or making them feel pressured. People know where you stand, so they are more inclined to trust you.

Conflict Resolution. This is your ability to uncover and manage differences in a positive and constructive manner. You don't let things fester. Rather, you help people reach agreement. Conflict is inevitable. It stems from divergent or opposing needs, ideas, beliefs, or goals and can lead to an unpleasant work dynamic and lowered productivity. When you can confront these challenging situations, you help people to strengthen their working relationships and create an environment more conducive to collaboration.

Influencing Others. This is your ability to persuade others to support your ideas and positions. Some people build influence through credibility, others through relationships, and still others through a combination of both. *Influencing Others* is probably one of the most difficult skills to master because of the complex nature of how humans operate and, frankly, the politicized landscape of most organizations. Everyone has his or her own set of interests. By *Influencing Others,* you create buy-in and gain cooperation from team members, colleagues, and senior leaders. You build your platform for future success.

Listening. This is your ability to make others feel they are being heard. You seek to understand others' points of view. You foster open communication and dialogue. *Listening* is the foundation of a number of other key skills like *Teamwork and Collaboration* and *Influencing Others.* Everyone wants to feel their opinions are taken seriously. Conversely, no one wants to work with a self-absorbed person who doesn't pay attention to the needs and interests of others. Exercising your *Listening* skills validates the people around you. As a result, they are more willing to hear what you have to say and work with you toward success.

Partnering and Relationship Building. This is your ability to develop interpersonal networks and build alliances. You collaborate across functions and departments. You respect individual and cultural differences. As the saying goes, "It's not what you do, it's who you know." *Partnering and Relationship Building* is about knowing the right people and developing a professional network built on mutual respect. To be effective, you must be able to influence, persuade, and gain acceptance of your ideas. When you are adept at *Partnering and Relationship Building,* half of your influencing work is already done.

Teamwork and Collaboration. This is your ability to work with others toward common goals or objectives. *Teamwork and Collaboration* creates an environment in which there is an open flow of information, a shared desire for success, and a willingness to step in to help others. Most organizations are interdependent systems laden with multiple reporting relationships, cross-functional committees, and matrixed structures. Modeling *Teamwork and Collaboration* in informal as well as formal teams is key to getting people to work together effectively and achieving results.

Verbal Communication. This is your ability to clearly and concisely articulate your thoughts. Your thought process is easy to follow. You enunciate your words and speak at the right volume and pace and with an inspiring tone. *Verbal Communication* skills enable you to convey information in a way that helps people to understand their roles and that reinforces your leadership capabilities.

Leading the Organization

This category of skills has to do with *your* ideas. What is your vision? How will you deploy it strategically? What level of risk are you willing to assume? We often find that this area does not get as much attention as it should because people are too busy putting out the fires directly in front of them to think strategically about the future. But how you lead the organization into the future is what will distinguish you from your competitors and put you on the path to success.

Creativity and Innovation. This is your ability to generate new ideas that improve performance and results. You challenge the status quo. You take mistakes and turn them into learning experiences that lead to better long-term outcomes. "Good enough" is never good enough. *Creativity and Innovation* are at the heart of every progressive organization. While the two go hand-in-hand, they are not the same. Your creativity is the source of the ideas from which you innovate to build new processes, technologies, products, goods, and services.

Entrepreneurship. This is your ability to boldly take the initiative. You view the world through the lens of possibility. You don't wait to be asked, and you are proactive in developing better business processes, products, or services. This is how you get ahead of the competition. Having an entrepreneurial mind-set opens doors to new opportunities where none existed before—all because you are ready to think differently, take risks, and, most important, act on your ideas.

External Awareness. This is your ability to identify the outside factors that affect your organization and then use this information in your work. You are the eyes and ears of the company. You keep up to date on international, national, industry, and social trends that could affect your team, department, and company. You use this information to best position the company to achieve a strategic competitive business advantage over both the short and long terms. Exercising *External Awareness* enables you to stay ahead of the curve and provide your organization with the information it needs to do the same.

Inspirational Vision. This is your ability to present a compelling future that drives performance. *Inspirational Vision* sets the emotional and motivational tone for the organization as a whole. When you operate with *Inspirational Vision,* the people around you are energized to achieve specific goals that align with the vision. They are clear on how their work contributes to making the vision a reality. In addition, the vision acts as a guiding light for people to make the best decisions for the organization on their own.

Organizational Awareness. This is your ability to understand how an organization functions, as well as the responsibilities, values, culture, standards, and practices that define its role and effectiveness in the marketplace. You are keenly aware of the organizational culture and are savvy to the political dynamics. You may not like everything you see, but you know how to work with it. The more aware you are of how decisions are made and the formal and informal rules that keep the organization fluid and cohesive, the more effective you will be in setting and achieving goals.

Service Motivation. This is your ability to serve others in the organization regardless of departments, roles, and reporting structure. You help others without expecting anything in return. You are instrumental in creating an organizational culture that encourages high-quality relationships with internal customers and colleagues. When you are motivated to serve, you increase the level of trust, and you foster a spirit of teamwork. In an environment that emphasizes service at all levels, people derive greater meaning and fulfillment from their professional lives.

Strategic Thinking. This is your ability to think five steps ahead. Your ideas may not be "visionary," but they are thought through in a way that is consistent with the overall direction of the organization and that supports its goals. Instead of focusing on the how-to aspects of management, *Strategic Thinking* is a broader, more long-term focus on what to do in terms of setting the direction for the organization, the team, and yourself. It helps you to identify threats and opportunities to the organization, the industry, and your career.

Leading Implementation

This category of skills is all about how you get things done—the execution of the strategy. Those who quickly climb the ranks demonstrate a strong ability to execute. One interesting thing we have noticed is that those with strong creativity, innovation, and vision skills tend to be weaker at execution and implementation, and vice versa. Strong leaders are able to excel at both categories of skills.

Coaching and Mentoring. This is your ability to help other people to solve their problems and increase their self-efficacy. Through coaching, you help others to shift their mind-sets, change behaviors, improve performance, and take accountability for their failures and successes. You help them to find their own answers. In contrast, you mentor by providing others with your personal insights into how they can be more effective. The combination of *Coaching and Mentoring* is extremely powerful in getting others to be more self-reliant and productive.

Customer Focus. This is your ability to serve your customers well. You know who your customers are, you understand their needs, and you do your best to bring their issues to resolution. Customers are the key to an organization's existence. They are also the most valuable source of information to grow and improve the business. When you demonstrate a *Customer Focus*, your customers become partners in your success, and vice versa. This powerful symbiotic relationship is critical to gaining a competitive edge in the marketplace.

Delegation. This is your ability to assign responsibilities to others to increase your and your team's productivity. You empower others to take ownership. You give them the opportunity to shine. *Delegation* is perhaps the most important skill when it comes to your productivity and value to the organization as a leader. The more effectively you delegate tasks to your team members, or others, the more available time you will have to strategize and develop new initiatives. The more you delegate, the more you can take on.

Effectiveness. This is your ability to get the job done well. You bring in the key stakeholders. You ensure that the right people are involved, and you keep everyone informed and on the right track through proactive communication. When you demonstrate *Effectiveness*, you are regarded as a go-to person in your organization—someone who can be counted on to deliver at a high level and to keep the organization's best interests in mind. The more effectively you perform your duties, the more valuable you are to the organization.

Monitoring Performance. This is your ability to measure and track the performance of staff, projects, and overall objectives. You communicate milestones, hold others accountable, and provide feedback and coaching. *Monitoring Performance* is important because life is full of surprises. The factors that are critical to a project's success can quickly change. In addition, people often misunderstand their roles and need guidance to stay on track and follow through. Without the tools and processes in place to monitor and manage performance, you put yourself at risk of blown budgets, delayed schedules, and even complete failures.

Planning and Organizing. This is your ability to conceive, develop, and implement plans to accomplish short- and long-term goals. You coordinate with other teams to ensure a thoughtful and systematic approach to everything from strategic forecasting to allocating resources to everyday scheduling. *Planning and Organizing* are key management skills; without them, nothing gets done.

Thoroughness. This is your ability to understand the direction in which you are headed and to focus on the details of how to get there. You understand how your goals fit into the organization's overall objectives, you plan out the steps you need to take, and you execute each with excellence. People trust that nothing slips by you and that you are always on top of things. Demonstrating *Thoroughness* requires the commitment to see a project to the end, the focus to complete each step, and the understanding of how each step contributes to the next. Your future success will be tied to your past *Thoroughness* time and again.

Now it is time for you to identify your Hidden Strengths! Complete the full assessment online at HiddenStrengths.com for a personalized report on your Hidden Strengths.

4

Reviewing Your Results

You might have a sense of what you naturally do really well, and you probably have an idea of the things you don't do well at all, but are you aware of the range of things that you do just okay? Imagine for a moment how many of those things you could be really good at with some focus and practice.

The Hidden Strengths Assessment does the hard work of identifying your skills in the middle so you can then take the steps to developing the ones most critical to your growth. Take a look at the skill rankings for George, the head of advertising sales at a publishing company, in Figure 3. The top-scoring items (i.e., the top 20 percent) were his Natural Strengths, whereas the bottom 10 percent were his Weaknesses. The items in between represented the gold mine of opportunity that lay in the middle 70 percent: his Hidden Strengths.

Year after year, George exceeded his numbers and received the company award for recognition of outstanding work. However, he felt his lack of attention to detail was holding him back from even better performance. His Hidden Strength report revealed that *Thoroughness* was in fact one of his lowest-ranking skills. In his middle range of skills were *Strategic Thinking* and *Inspirational Vision*, among others. He had some really great ideas for how to move the company from medium- to top-tier territory, but he had neither the time nor the discipline to create a compelling message and road map to convince others. His lack of *Thoroughness* was a real deterrent to his sitting down, creating a plan, and doing the pitch, and he wasn't delegating anyone to pick up his slack.

▼ Item Scores

(Excludes Self)

MEAN

Partnering and Relationship Building
Emotional Control
Delegation
Teamwork and Collaboration
Flexibility
Assertiveness
Customer Focus
Entrepreneurship
Verbal Communication
Resilience
Strategic Thinking
Organizational Awareness
Listening
Self-Confidence
Service Motivation
Conflict Resolution
Executive Presence
Influencing Others
Integrity
External Awareness
Creativity and Innovation
Inspirational Vision
Effectiveness
Work/Life Balance
Coaching and Mentoring
Monitoring Performance
Planning and Organizing
Thoroughness

Figure 3. George's Hidden Strengths Assessment—Skill Rankings

When George finally hired someone to handle his Weaknesses, he had more time to work on his ideas about how to move the company forward. He took the focus off his Weaknesses and concentrated on his Hidden Strengths. By eliminating having to manage the minutiae of his job, he had a much greater impact on the company's future.

Your Hidden Strengths Report

The first step in reviewing your Hidden Strengths report is looking at the section that lists the skills in your top 20 percent—your Natural Strengths. These higher-scoring skills should not surprise you. They are typically not only the skills you feel you do very well but the ones you use most often.

Think about the connections between these skills. Do you see any patterns? For example, do most of them belong to a specific skill category, such as Leading Others? Do they mostly relate to the ideas you have and how you talk about them (i.e., Leading the Organization), or are they more clustered around how you demonstrate *Integrity* and *Emotional Control* (i.e., Leading Self)?

It is time to determine the story that the data are telling you. Don't get caught up in exactly where the top 20 percent ends. Instead, look at the skills as clusters within the four skill categories: Leading Self, Leading Others, Leading the Organization, and Leading Implementation. Which have you become overly dependent on in your current role?

Next, take a look at your Hidden Strengths—the ones that fall in the middle 70 percent or so of your skill set. Again, look for patterns in the data. What clusters of skills are you seeing? Can you find any clusters related to your ability to Leading Implementation in your organization? When it comes to Leading Others, are you strong at *Partnering and Relationship Building* but just okay at *Influencing Others*? This may mean that people like working with you but you are not doing enough to leverage those relationships to push for new ideas.

Reflecting on your short- and long-term professional goals, are there any Hidden Strengths that you should immediately begin developing?

Which of the twenty or so skills that fall into your middle range should be your first targets for turning into Learned Strengths?

Finally, let's examine your Weaknesses—the bottom 10 percent of skills that seem to be a no-go no matter how hard you try. Remember the bandage approach to managing your Weaknesses. Which of these skills can you avoid doing at all? Which can you delegate? What about the ones you absolutely can't ignore? Can you spend a minimum amount of time on them to become proficient enough to get by?

Now that you have completed and reviewed your assessment, let's proceed to the final part of the book to learn how you can create your own Hidden Strengths Development Plan.

PART THREE

Harnessing Your Potential

It's time to move from "I should really do this" to "Here's how I'm going to develop myself." Part 3 provides a five-step action plan for turning your Hidden Strengths into Learned Strengths. It concludes with some final words on how you can use the Hidden Strengths methodology to constantly evolve in your profession and as a leader.

5

Making Your Hidden Strengths Work for You

So you've completed your Hidden Strengths assessment and learned about the twenty or so skills that fall into your middle range (if you haven't gone online to do the assessment yet, what are you waiting for?). Don't worry—you don't have to work on all twenty skills at the same time. In fact, we don't recommend it. Rather, we have provided a five-step action plan for identifying and developing the Hidden Strengths that are aligned with your current professional objectives.

At the end of your Hidden Strengths report, you will find a guide to help you think through and create your personal Hidden Strengths Development Plan. You can also find an easy-to-use worksheet that summarizes the five steps in the Appendix.

Hidden Strengths Development Plan

1. Find your motivation.
2. Identify your goals.
3. Choose your Hidden Strengths to develop.
4. Turn your Hidden Strengths into Learned Strengths.
5. Evaluate your progress.

Step 1: Find Your Motivation

Before you embark upon this Hidden Strengths journey, there is one final question you need to ask yourself: Why am I doing this?

Table 2 Sources of Motivation

Security	Identity	Stimulation
Compensation and Benefits: Making enough money to pay the bills.	*Organizational Identity:* Feeling connected to the organization and being able to tell friends and family that we work for a great company, doing great things in the world.	*New and Different:* Being drawn to cool, new projects.
Job Security: Doing our jobs and ensuring we won't get fired tomorrow.	*Self:* Being recognized for the contributions we are making and feeling a sense of personal pride in our work.	*Mastery:* More than just learning a new skill but achieving a level of mastery that strengthens our resumes and marketability.

Knowing your source of motivation is what will help you to commit to the behavioral changes necessary to develop your Hidden Strengths.

When we talk to leaders, the topic of motivation often comes up. That's because most people say they want to improve but don't make the effort to change. This is a cold and hard fact. Think about how many people say they want to lose weight and get into shape, but they don't do anything about it. Another fact: Developing Hidden Strengths requires ongoing effort and a commitment to growth. You can't just give up if you have a bad day. By keeping what motivates you up front, you will be more dedicated and disciplined in your efforts to grow.

Based on fifteen-plus years of coaching experience and closely observing human behavior in the workplace, we have identified three critical sources of motivation: security, identity, and stimulation (Table 2). We highly recommend exploring these sources to find which resonates with you.

Security. According to Maslow's Hierarchy of Needs, a well-established model of human motivation, we are first driven to satisfy basic needs like food, shelter, and safety.[11] In the context of the workplace, safety (i.e., security) can be further categorized into compensation and job security. You may want to take the next step in your career so you can better support yourself and your family. Alternately, your motivation to be a top performer may be that the next time a recession hits, your employer will be more inclined to keep you around.

Identity. As social creatures, we are driven by the need to connect with the things we care about. Because we spend most of our lifetimes working, a huge source of motivation is feeling proud of the company we work for and the impact we will make on the world. When we believe we are on a winning team, we are motivated to contribute to the company's continued success. Personally, we also want to be recognized for our contributions. Sometimes motivation comes in the form of a higher title that establishes our identity as a top performer. We put in the necessary work to get that promotion and title.

Stimulation. We all desire to be challenged and stimulated. In the workplace, we are constantly on the lookout for new and exciting opportunities that keep us engaged and encourage us to grow. These new opportunities can manifest themselves as new and "cool" projects or initiatives, or new roles. When it comes to new roles, gaining mastery in a new domain is another extremely powerful source of motivation. It is only when we master a skill that we feel we are doing our best and have a sense of autonomy.

When you try new behaviors, practice new skills, and invest the time in yourself to grow, you should have an understanding of why you are doing those things. You need to make sure the reasons for change are meaningful and sustainable for you. Define for yourself your sources of motivation to ensure you stay committed to developing your Hidden Strengths.

Step 2: Identify Your Goals

What are the goals you are working toward in your current position? For example, have you been tasked with driving innovation within your team because the competition is leaving you in the dust? Or are you being asked to effectively execute your company's strategy to reach your sales targets?

In the next year, what do you need to do to move up? Make sure the goals you are responsible for align with the higher-level goals of your organization, department, and team. Tie them to the larger vision and company strategy to ensure that what you spending your time and energy on will have an impact.

Last, which category or categories of skills—Leading Self, Leading Others, Leading the Organization, or Leading Implementation—will be necessary to achieve these goals? Be as specific as possible as you answer these questions. They hold the key to determining the right Hidden Strengths on which to focus.

Step 3: Choose Your Hidden Strengths to Develop

Now it's time to link your motivation to what you hope to achieve and the Hidden Strengths you can leverage to do so. As we discussed in Chapter 4, start by looking for any patterns in your middle range of skills. Can you find clusters of two or three skills in certain categories like Leading Self or in specific themes like communication or vision?

Grouping your middle skills into clusters helps you to find the ones that support your goals and complement one another. For example, within the theme of communication, you may find that if you get stronger at *Listening* (Leading Others), it will also help you build stronger *Coaching and Mentoring* skills (Leading Implementation) for your team so they can get more things done. Or you may find that if you start practicing *Resilience*, your *Self-Confidence* begins to rise, making you that much stronger at Leading Self, the category of skills you have identified as necessary to achieve your goals over the next year.

Choosing which Hidden Strengths to develop is uniquely personal. The process is entirely dependent on the clusters of skills present in your middle range as well as on your goals. A one-size-fits-all approach does not exist. However, here are three examples that illustrate how this crucial step can be carried out.

Example 1: John, Senior Director

Hidden Strengths Cluster: Partnering and Relationship Building
    and Assertiveness
Skill Category: Leading Others

John was a very senior leader in the organization, with five direct reports who had 150 engineers under them. John had very strong technical skills as a hardware engineer, but he was often quiet in meetings, and people had trouble understanding where he stood on various issues. This was a big problem because John was responsible for some next-generation technology that was being developed with another department that had a reputation for being difficult to work with.

John would occasionally volunteer information at meetings, but his manager had to ask him direct questions to find out what he was thinking. However, on the few occasions that John did offer his opinion, his comments were very well thought out. When we met with John, he explained that he didn't like to say things just for the sake of posturing or calling attention to himself. He didn't realize that his humility came across as boredom, and his lack of communication was undermining his credibility as a leader.

We began with an assessment of John's leadership skills. The results revealed that *Thoroughness* was a Natural Strength, one of his highest-scoring skills (Figure 4). John had an eye for detail, and up to this point, his ability to execute was the most significant reason for his success at the company. However, relying too much on this default tendency was becoming detrimental to his longer-term success.

At the bottom of John's assessment was a cluster of skills that included *Delegation* and *Coaching and Mentoring*. Assigning more tasks to his direct reports and adopting a more hands-off management style were growing increasingly critical to John's success as he took on more responsibility. However, in the short term, these lowest-scoring skills were serving him well because when he did handle things himself, it kept him in the loop. He was expected to know all the details and be ready to talk about them in the weekly executive reviews.

The assessment also revealed a cluster of skills in John's middle range that included *Partnering and Relationship Building* and *Assertiveness*. Given John's new assignment, a correlation between these Hidden Strengths emerged. If John were more assertive in meetings, people would be more aware of his participation in the project. They would also know where he stood on technical principles, ideas, and decisions, which would increase their trust in his judgment. A growing reservoir of trust in John's intentions and an understanding of his thought process would help to strengthen his relationship with the other department.

Thus, John focused his time and energy on reframing what it meant for him to actively participate. He worked on finding his voice and position on issues and getting over his fear that others would think he was grandstanding. Over the course of three months, people could see a marked improvement in John's performance. His manager appreciated that he was much more engaged in meetings and contributed more to the conversation. After six months, his relationships with his peers were much stronger. More important, the department he was working with trusted him more because he was forthright about his opinions, and they could tell he was on the same wavelength. Eventually, other teams specifically requested that John work with them on their projects. He developed a reputation for dedication and hard work, and he was promoted a short time later.

John could have spent an inordinate amount of time focused on his implementation skills and delegating and coaching the five

▼ Item Scores

(Excludes Self)

MEAN

Effectiveness

Thoroughness

Resilience

Integrity

Emotional Control

Self-Confidence

Customer Focus

Organizational Awareness

Strategic Thinking

Monitoring Performance

Listening

Assertiveness

Teamwork and Collaboration

Partnering and Relationship Building

Executive Presence

Flexibility

Planning and Organizing

External Awareness

Creativity and Innovation

Entrepreneurship

Service Motivation

Conflict Resolution

Verbal Communication

Influencing Others

Inspirational Vision

Work/Life Balance

Delegation

Coaching and Mentoring

Figure 4. John's Hidden Strengths Assessment—Skill Rankings

leaders who reported to him. However, this would not have made a significant immediate impact on his goals of getting the new technology developed and delivered with the other department. Of course, this doesn't mean that *Delegation* and *Coaching and Mentoring* are not important skills. As with everything in life, John had to prioritize his leadership development efforts and pick the skills that would take him the farthest—his Hidden Strengths of *Partnering and Relationship Building* and *Assertiveness*. The most effective use of his time was focusing on putting himself out there so others could see the value of his contributions and insights.

Example 2: Barry, CEO
Hidden Strengths Cluster: Resilience, Flexibility, and Delegation
Skill Categories: Leading Self and Leading Implementation

Barry was an executive who left a Fortune 100 company to start his own business.

Barry's 360-degree assessment revealed his Natural Strengths in the areas of *Creativity and Innovation, Entrepreneurship, External Awareness,* and *Assertiveness* (Figure 5). This made sense: Barry had left a big company because he wanted to do things differently, and he had some great ideas about how he could make it all happen.

What showed up as his Weaknesses were *Emotional Control, Coaching and Mentoring,* and *Listening.* Sometimes Barry's passion and drive (i.e., his *Assertiveness*) got the best of him. When others didn't understand his ideas or position on an issue, he would get upset and just stop talking. Barry acknowledged that he was short-tempered at times, but he also knew that his passion was a major driver of his success. So although the awareness was there, it was really hard for him to do something about it. Barry had also gotten

▼ Item Scores

(Excludes Self)

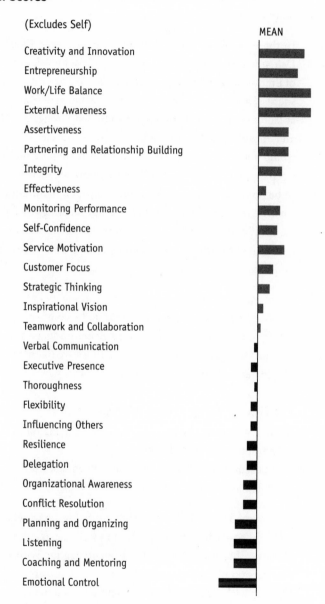

Figure 5. Barry's Hidden Strengths Assessment—Skill Rankings

so used to doing things himself that he found it hard to rely on his more junior team.

In the middle of Barry's skill set were *Resilience*, *Flexibility*, and *Delegation*. We noticed a connection. We acknowledged that lack of Emotional Control was detrimental to Barry's future leadership success, but instead of attacking this Weakness directly, we looked at factors that could help build his Hidden Strengths of *Resilience* and *Flexibility*. If Barry learned to be more flexible and resilient, he would not get so fired up that he lost control of his emotions. More sleep would help him control his stress level and increase his ability to be *resilient*, which in turn would help him maintain *Emotional Control*. If he prepared ahead of time for meetings by formulating his ideas and alternatives, it would make him more flexible when he listened to others' ideas, and everyone would feel heard and understood.

Barry was rarely in the office to do *Coaching and Mentoring*. This was one of his Weaknesses, however, so he compensated by delegating more to his team. They were given the space to make their own mistakes and learn from them. This gave Barry the opportunity to deal with bigger issues, so it was a win-win.

Example 3: Jessica, Vice President
Hidden Strengths Cluster: Planning and Organizing, Effectiveness, Thoroughness, and Strategic Thinking
Skill Categories: Leading the Organization and Leading Implementation

Jessica was known in her company for being smart, efficient, and quick. She was also approachable and well respected by her team. However, her organization had been struggling with releasing a new version of their product that had more features. They would come up with ideas, start working on them, and then go back to the drawing board when they hit some bumps in an effort to be responsive to potential issues. In the end, not much got delivered because of the frequent changes in direction. Jessica blamed herself for not being a strong visionary and for being unsure about where the team should be focusing their energy.

When we conducted the 360-degree assessment on Jessica, it was clear that her Natural Strengths were in the areas of *Emotional Control, Resilience, Flexibility, Listening,* and *Delegation* (Figure 6). Her Weaknesses lay in *Creativity and Innovation, Influencing Others,* and *Inspirational Vision.* This was not surprising given her communication issues. She had difficulty coming up with good ideas, and she wasn't able to convince others of a firm plan because she was too easily swayed (i.e., flexible) and tried to listen to everyone. She didn't seem to have a lot of confidence in her own ideas.

Jessica's Hidden Strengths included *Planning and Organizing, Effectiveness, Thoroughness,* and *Strategic Thinking.* This told us that she needed a thinking partner to address her Weaknesses.

It was obvious that Jessica needed a clear and compelling vision. We knew, however, that *Inspirational Vision* would never be one of her strengths. She needed someone to brainstorm with and think through the possibilities for the future. Visionary ideas must come at the beginning of a project. Only after there is a decision to move forward do we lay out resources and milestones, consider potential roadblocks, and create contingency plans.

In reality, most of us don't think up grand ideas in a vacuum. When Jessica agreed to take on a thinking partner to periodically check in to address her weaknesses, it gave her more space to work on developing her Hidden Strengths of *Strategic Thinking, Planning and Organizing, Thoroughness,* and *Effectiveness.* She became highly competent at following up with her leaders on how things were progressing and working with them to remove roadblocks. Because they were strategic in how they planned and approached any

▼ Item Scores

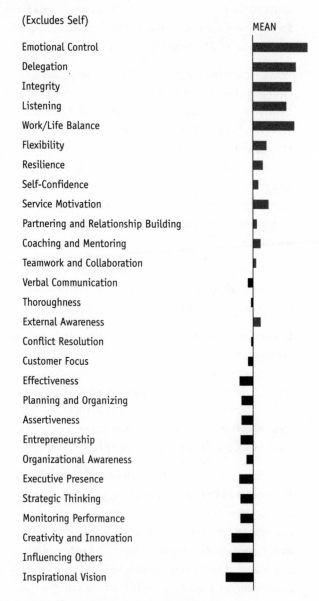

(Excludes Self)

MEAN

Emotional Control
Delegation
Integrity
Listening
Work/Life Balance
Flexibility
Resilience
Self-Confidence
Service Motivation
Partnering and Relationship Building
Coaching and Mentoring
Teamwork and Collaboration
Verbal Communication
Thoroughness
External Awareness
Conflict Resolution
Customer Focus
Effectiveness
Planning and Organizing
Assertiveness
Entrepreneurship
Organizational Awareness
Executive Presence
Strategic Thinking
Monitoring Performance
Creativity and Innovation
Influencing Others
Inspirational Vision

Figure 6. Jessica's Hidden Strengths Assessment—Skill Rankings

issues that arose, the team was finally able to focus on executing their original ideas and getting the new features to market. Then, once the market responded, they could work effectively to make improvements as necessary.

Step 4: Turn Your Hidden Strengths into Learned Strengths

Now that you've determined which two or three Hidden Strengths to focus on, it's time to figure out the old behaviors you have to change and the new behaviors you need to adopt to turn them into Learned Strengths. The following resources can help.

Your Manager. Use your next one-on-one with your manager to discuss your goals and the Hidden Strengths you will use to achieve them. Ask for feedback on the kinds of behaviors that they would like to see you demonstrate in order to help you master those skills. If you feel as if this is something you can't discuss with your manager, find someone else in your workplace with whom you interact regularly.

Your Human Resources Department. If you are in a larger company, talk with your HR department to see what classes they offer or can make available to you.

Your Own Research. It is always important to do your own research. A simple online search will lead you to an exhaustive number of websites, blogs, articles, and books geared toward developing specific skills. Some of our favorites include the *Harvard Business Review* and online bookstore searches. In addition to the vast trove of resources accessible on the Internet, SkylineG.com also lists many free resources for additional learning.

Practice Everywhere. Every interaction in your workplace is an opportunity to practice skill development. Presentations, meetings, one-on-ones, emails, proposals, hallway conversations—these are all practice opportunities. You control how you come across in all of these interactions.

If you are working on developing *Listening* skills, for example, every conversation is an opportunity to practice. If you are focused on exercising your *Entrepreneurship* skills, every decision you make is an opportunity to ask yourself, "How can I be more proactive or take a more aggressive approach in this situation?"

People need to see you consistently demonstrating a skill if they are going to change their minds about what kind of leader you are. Remember that "they" are always watching you. It might sound creepy, but it's true. In the context of the workplace, "they" includes anyone who has an influence on your success—from managers and direct reports to cross-functional partners. Every interaction (or lack thereof) leaves an impression.

John leveraged his daily meetings to practice voicing his position. He needed to be consistent for two reasons: to get to a point where the behavior felt more natural to him *and* to get people to notice and believe that his newly developed *Assertiveness* was intentional and here to stay.

Step 5: Evaluate Your Progress

It is through the processes of evaluating and re-evaluating that you really start to refine your skills. After every interaction, ask yourself these questions: How could it have gone better? What did I learn? What should I do differently the next time?

Getting feedback from others is extremely helpful in evaluating progress; it can be a much-needed reality check. Additionally, talking with others about the changes you are attempting to make can be a source of renewed motivation. Any new endeavor is hard. When you get positive reinforcement from others that you are making progress, it motivates you to keep going.

Finally, when you discuss your progress with others ask them for their observations and specific stories of your new behavior. When people share their new stories about how you have grown and developed, they overwrite the old stories in their minds. These new stories start to shift the way the ecosystem (i.e., your managers, peers, direct reports, etc.) starts to see you. Sharing your journey of turning Hidden

Strengths into Learned Strengths highlights your determination to keep on growing and learning. It is a point of admiration and respect and tunes people into the positive changes you have been making. Then when you ask for feedback, they are more apt to recognize your hard work. Your professional story becomes one of ongoing positive change and the impact you are making. This is what they will remember about you and what they will tell others about you. After all, it would be a shame if you worked so hard to grow and no one noticed.

When you ask for feedback, give context, and be specific about what you want to know. For example, if you ask for feedback on your *Listening* skills, say, "As you know, I'm working on honing my listening skills. Do you think the other team felt that I understood their concerns?" Don't just ask something vague like, "How am I doing?" You want the person to give you actionable advice and have specific details that they can take to others about the progress you are making. Which response would be more helpful to you: "Yes, you're doing great" or "Yes, I could tell they believed you took their concerns seriously when you explained the problem from their point of view"?

6

Leading Your Evolution

I f there's only one thing you take from this book, we hope it is this: You are so much more than what comes naturally to you. Within you lies a gold mine of Hidden Strengths just waiting to be unleashed. Don't discount this treasure trove of opportunity lying just beneath the surface. With awareness and dedication, you can leverage these Hidden Strengths to continually reach new levels of performance and success.

Did you know that self-awareness is a key factor in high-performance and long-term career success?[12] According to a study by the Korn/Ferry Institute, one way we frequently undermine our potential is by being ignorant of our skills. By taking a narrow view of our capabilities and relying too much on skills we've had for many years, we can become "obsolete."[13] Don't keep your Hidden Strengths hidden. Assessments, feedback, and practice can help you realize your potential to improve. This ongoing evolution is the cornerstone of the Hidden Strengths methodology.

Sustainability

With time and practice, the skills you've focused on will become easier. Although they will never be your Natural Strengths, they will come to you more naturally. Remember, these Hidden Strengths did not automatically appear at the top of your skill set. Through your own effort, you turned them into Learned Strengths, and you must continue to practice them to keep them fresh.

After a few months, take another look at your personal Hidden Strengths Development Plan. What progress have you made? What more do you need to do to master those skills? The acquisition of skills and expertise occurs mostly through experience and training.[14] Don't let your new Learned Strengths atrophy from lack of use. The minute you become complacent, you start getting yourself into trouble. Keep up the good work!

The Never-Ending Adventure

Learning is a lifelong endeavor. Once you have mastered your first round of Learned Strengths, look to see what's next. After all, you have at least seventeen or eighteen more skills to go! Research shows that leaders and aspiring leaders who are open to growth and change and eager for continuous development are more likely to be promoted.[15] And as good old Benjamin Franklin put it, "When you're finished changing, you're finished."

Use the five-step Hidden Strengths Development Plan in Chapter 5 to identify and develop a new cluster of skills based on your professional goals. And when you've mastered those, shampoo, rinse, and repeat!

Share the Love

Whatever your title, if you are performing at the top of your game, you are a role model. This gives you the opportunity (and the responsibility) to help others grow along with you—for their personal development as well as for the continued success of your organization.

Inspire those around you with your story of growth and your mastery of new Learned Strengths. Encourage your team and colleagues to find their own Hidden Strengths to unleash. Embrace the leader inside of you, and start a professional development revolution!

Appendix A
The Twenty-Eight Skills and Why They Matter

Table 3 The Twenty-Eight Skills

Category	Skill
Leading Self	
	Emotional Control
	Flexibility
	Integrity
	Resilience
	Self-Confidence
	Executive Presence
	Work/Life Balance
Leading Others	
	Assertiveness
	Conflict Resolution
	Influencing Others
	Listening
	Partnering and Relationship Building
	Teamwork and Collaboration
	Verbal Communication
Leading the Organization	
	Creativity and Innovation
	Entrepreneurship
	External Awareness
	Inspirational Vision
	Organizational Awareness
	Service Motivation
	Strategic Thinking
Leading Implementation	
	Coaching and Mentoring
	Customer Focus
	Delegation
	Effectiveness
	Monitoring Performance
	Planning and Organizing
	Thoroughness

Leading Self

This category covers how you regulate the kind of person you want to be as a leader and a professional. When you know who you are and can control your emotions, you exude a quiet confidence that inspires others. These skills may appear more like natural talents or traits, but they can be learned. We have worked with thousands of leaders to help them build stronger skills in these areas, and you can do it, too!

Emotional Control

Emotional Control is the ability to maintain a professional, respectful attitude during stressful situations. Leaders who operate with high levels of *Emotional Control* are masters of their reactions. They remain composed instead of letting their emotions get the best of them and acting reflexively in ways that can damage both relationships with others and their reputations.

Why it's important: The more *Emotional Control* you demonstrate, the more approachable and credible you become. We are more willing to follow leaders who are in control of themselves and their emotions. The fear is that reactive leaders may take us down one path when they are upset and then change their mind later when they calm down. As a leader and a high-performing professional, you want others to trust that no matter what happens, you can keep your cool and handle any situation that comes at you.

Flexibility

Flexible leaders can bend without breaking. They are open to change and new information, willingly compromising instead of sticking rigidly to positions that are no longer viable. Flexible leaders do not get "stuck" when a solution doesn't work or when changes are needed; rather, they immediately begin to find possible alternatives that best meet the needs of their teams, stakeholders, and the business.

Why it's important: Change is the only constant—today and forever. Organizations must adapt quickly to meet the changing needs of the marketplace and stay competitive. Flexible leaders who can respond judiciously to shifting conditions and unexpected difficulties are more successful. *Flexibility* is a skill that will help you remain relevant and contribute in a meaningful way regardless of your role and professional ambitions.

Integrity

Integrity is a state of alignment between a leader's beliefs, values, and actions. Leaders who demonstrate *Integrity* have high standards of ethics and fairness. They can be counted on to do the "right thing" for their teams and the organization. They are perceived as incorruptible.

Why it's important: If you cannot be trusted, you will never be effective. *Integrity* instills trust. People are more willing to follow people who show *Integrity* because they trust that their best interests are at heart. If your thoughts, words, and actions are in alignment, the people around you will feel a sense of security that will help them to buy into your ideas and direction.

Resilience

Resilience is the mental, emotional, and physical stamina required to deal with adverse and stressful circumstances, while still performing effectively. A resilient leader maintains focus and optimism under less than ideal circumstances, always looking for ways to turn disruptions into growth opportunities.

Why it's important: Reorganizations, downsizings, mergers, budget pressures, and job insecurity are just a few of the high-stress, high-pressure conditions that can throw you off center in today's business climate. When you can summon your *Resilience* to manage through tough times in a productive manner, you show that you can be trusted to take on higher levels of responsibility.

Self-Confidence

Self-Confidence is the expression of your belief in your own abilities. It is not arrogance. Confident leaders know they have what it takes to get the job done. This is demonstrated through the clarity and conviction in their words and actions.

Why it's important: If you can express your thoughts directly and with confidence, you will have more influence over others. When you show that you believe in your ability to lead a team, manage a project, or complete a job successfully, others are motivated to believe in you as well.

Executive Presence

Leaders with *Executive Presence* command the room by displaying poise, authenticity, competence, and commitment. They project their thoughts and ideas in ways that inspire trust and compel others to action. They willingly take the driver's seat and are trusted to set the direction for what comes next.

Why it's important: *Executive Presence* is the essence of leadership. It is earned authority. When you exercise *Executive Presence*, you command the attention and respect of those around you, allowing you to more easily gain buy-in on your ideas. You project an image of authentic confidence and competence that makes others want to follow your lead. This is what makes *Executive Presence* one of the most vital business skills you can develop and master.

Work/Life Balance

Work/Life Balance is the equilibrium you achieve between the professional and personal aspects of your life. While balance is typically considered a 50:50 ratio, true *Work/Life Balance* is subjective and dynamic. The ratios differ for different people and for different times in their lives. Leaders who achieve *Work/Life Balance* feel they are spending quality time and energy in both spheres of life without feeling resentful about the choices they inevitably have to make between the two.

Why it's important: Developing the skill of *Work/Life Balance* allows you to stay engaged in both areas of your life so you can easily switch focus from one to the other without getting depleted. It also helps to avoid frustration from work spilling over into your personal life, or vice versa. Long-term professional success requires that you don't resent the time you spend at work versus at home. Practicing *Work/Life Balance* is the key to a healthy lifestyle and a sustainable and fulfilling livelihood that adds to your sense of identity, accomplishment, and contribution in the world.

Leading Others

This category of skills is about how you relate to others and form strong working relationships. We find that this area can be particularly hard for people who are more results oriented and focused on the end product. The thing to remember is that almost all projects are a team effort and results cannot be achieved by one person alone. Relating well to people and managing their expectations and needs are essential parts of the process that cannot be overlooked.

Assertiveness

Assertive leaders are direct without being aggressive. They can express their points clearly without inserting a negative emotional component. Instead of backing down when opposing views are presented or sticking rigidly to their convictions, assertive leaders listen to what others have to say with the intent of having an open exchange of ideas and reaching a conclusion that works for all parties.

Why it's important: When you exercise *Assertiveness*, you state your opinions in a way that engages others and doesn't put them on the defensive or make them feel pressured to agree with you. People not only know where you stand, but they know you welcome their opinions as well. This makes them more inclined to trust you and be influenced by your ideas.

Conflict Resolution

Conflict Resolution is the ability to uncover and resolve disagreements in a positive and constructive manner. Leaders who excel at *Conflict Resolution* do not let disputes fester for very long; they are focused on helping people reach an agreement and nurturing strong working relationships.

Why it's important: Conflict stems from divergent or opposing needs, ideas, beliefs, or goals. It is inevitable and can quickly lead to discord. Unresolved conflict creates an unpleasant and awkward working environment that can be detrimental to a team's productivity. When you practice *Conflict Resolution*, you create the space for open dialogue and allow all parties to feel validated. When people feel heard, they are more inclined to work collaboratively toward common goals.

Influencing Others

Leaders with strong influencing skills create buy-in and support for their ideas by building consensus. They have strong persuasive skills that they use to highlight their credibility. They are also strong relationship builders who are able to gain the cooperation of others to support them in their goals. Everyone has his or her own personal interests. Influential leaders understand the needs of others and their underlying positions and can use this knowledge to find common ground and goals.

Why it's important: *Influencing Others* is probably one of the most difficult skills to master because of the complex nature of how humans operate and, frankly, the political landscape of most organizations. However, when you can exercise your influence, you begin to build your platform for future success. The more support and cooperation you get from others, the higher your chances are of achieving your goals.

Listening

Leaders who have strong *Listening* skills seek to understand others' points of views by fostering open communication and dialogue. They show curiosity and ask questions to ensure that others feel heard. They gain influence by building strong working relationships based on a mutual respect for one another's opinions.

Why it's important: This skill set is the foundation to a number of related skills like *Teamwork and Collaboration* and *Influencing Others*. Everyone wants to be taken seriously, and no one likes a self-absorbed person who doesn't pay attention to the needs and interests of others. In addition, strong *Listening* skills can give you an important competitive advantage because you are privy to more valuable knowledge and feedback than those who do not seek the counsel of others. Although we may emphasize problem solving in our day-to-day activities, the working relationships we build and the way we make people feel are just as important to long-term success.

Partnering and Relationship Building

Partnering and Relationship Building is the ability to develop interpersonal networks and to build alliances. Leaders who are strong in this skill respect individual and cultural differences and are good at collaborating across functions and departments. They are able to create and sustain connections with those they work with and have worked with in the past.

Why it's important: It is common wisdom that "it's not what you do, it's who you know." *Partnering and Relationship Building* is about knowing the right people and developing professional networks built on mutual respect and trust. In today's business world, "command and control" leadership doesn't always work. Increasingly, individuals find themselves working in matrixed organizations and responding to multiple internal and external customers. As a consequence, your effectiveness is directly related to your ability to influence, persuade, and gain buy-in for your ideas and initiatives. When you are adept at partnering and building long-term working relationships, half of your influencing work is already done.

Teamwork and Collaboration

Teamwork and Collaboration is the ability to work with others toward a set of common goals or objectives. Working collaboratively in the context of a team means there are multidirectional flows of information, a shared desire to have everyone succeed, and a willingness to step in to help others when necessary.

Why it's important: Success in business is rarely ever achieved by one person or one department alone. The ability to work well together in formal and informal teams is crucial, especially in teams with interdependent goals and objectives. Modeling *Teamwork and Collaboration* is critical to encouraging this behavior in those you work with. When teams are aligned in their values and goals, the result is a heightened sense of commitment and trust and increased productivity.

Verbal Communication

Verbal Communication is the ability to clearly articulate thoughts and opinions to others in an organized and succinct manner. Whether in informal daily communications or formal presentations, leaders with strong *Verbal Communication* skills are logical in their thought processes; clearly enunciate their words; and speak at a volume, tone, and pace that are engaging.

Why it's important: Practicing your *Verbal Communication* skills helps you to convey information in ways that help people to understand their roles and that reinforce your leadership capabilities. Strong communication skills are a direct route to gaining influence and acceptance, especially in face-to-face meetings.

Leading the Organization

This category of skills has to do with *your* ideas. What is your vision? How will you deploy it strategically? What level of risk are you willing to assume? Often, this area does not get the attention it should because leaders worry more about the here and now than about the future. How you lead the organization into the future, however, is what will distinguish you from your competitors and put you on the path to success.

Creativity and Innovation

Creativity is the ability to generate new ideas, new ways of doing things, and new solutions. Innovation is the ability to implement these ideas and solutions to improve performance or results. Leaders that exhibit *Creativity and Innovation* challenge the status quo by never accepting "good enough." They see mistakes as learning experiences that lead to stronger, long-term outcomes.

Why it's important: *Creativity and Innovation* is at the heart of any progressive organization. Individuals and businesses need plenty of both to be competitive in today's rapidly changing work environment. Your acts of creativity generate the ideas and concepts from which you will innovate to build new, more successful technologies, products, goods, and services.

Entrepreneurship

Entrepreneurial leaders are willing to take risks to achieve a recognized benefit for the organization. They view the world through the lens of possibility and are proactive in taking the initiative to develop better business processes, products, and services. They do not wait around to be asked but simply assume the responsibility to move things forward. An entrepreneurial mind-set requires agility, adaptability, and a readiness to respond at a moment's notice with concrete action, while remaining open to a variety of options.

Why it's important: *Entrepreneurship* is an exciting foundational skill for generating and seizing opportunities that can improve performance, bring ideas to life, and put you ahead of the competition. Having an entrepreneurial mind-set opens the door to new business processes, products, services, and market possibilities where none existed before—all because you are ready to think differently, take risks, and, most important, act on your ideas.

External Awareness

External Awareness is the ability to identify the outside factors that impact a company and using this information efficiently. Externally aware leaders are up to date on the international, national, industry, and social trends that affect their teams, departments, and organizations. They use this information for both short-term and long-range plans to achieve strategic competitive business advantages.

Why it's important: Staying inwardly focused in a world that is constantly changing is dangerous. Vigilant *External Awareness* enables you to proactively determine which new moves or policy and process changes you and your organization need to make to stay ahead of the curve. You might think of practicing *External Awareness* as being the eyes and ears of the company. This is how you stay relevant in your position and gain the trust of others to take on higher levels of responsibility.

Inspirational Vision

A shared *Inspirational Vision* helps others to understand the organization's direction. Visionary leaders present a compelling future state that drives their teams to perform at their best and get excited about the future. They inspire people to come to work every day and act in ways that will make the vision a reality.

Why it's important: *Inspirational Vision* sets the emotional and motivational tone for the organization as a whole. When you demonstrate *Inspirational Vision*, you motivate your team to achieve specific goals that align with the vision. They are clear on how their work contributes to making the vision a reality—and they are excited about it. In addition, the vision acts as a guiding light for people to make the best decisions for the organization on their own.

Organizational Awareness

Organizational Awareness is the ability to see and understand all aspects of how an organization functions, as well as the responsibilities, values, culture, standards, and practices that define the organization's role and effectiveness in the marketplace. Organizationally aware leaders are savvy to the full scope of political dynamics in the workplace. They may not like everything they see, but they know how to work with it and use it to their professional advantage.

Why it's important: It is impossible to be fully effective in the marketplace without understanding how you are bringing products, services, and initiatives to the table. The more aware you are of how the decision makers work, how teams and departments join forces, and the formal and informal rules that keep the organization fluid and cohesive, the more successful you will be in setting and achieving goals and objectives. Without *Organizational Awareness*, it is difficult, if not impossible, to create a collaborative working environment and a viable long-term strategy.

Service Motivation

Service Motivation is a commitment to serving others in the organization across departments, roles, and reporting structures. Leaders who practice *Service Motivation* take the initiative to help others without expecting anything in return. They are instrumental in creating an organizational culture that encourages high-quality relationships with internal customers and colleagues.

Why it's important: We all want to be treated with kindness and generosity. When you act in service of others, it fosters a spirit of teamwork and mutual respect that leads to strong long-term working relationships. It makes people to want to work with you when you demonstrate that you can think beyond yourself. Service to internal customers, colleagues, and the organization as a whole is an important skill you can practice on a daily basis.

Strategic Thinking

Strategic Thinking is about thinking five steps ahead. Strategic leaders are not necessarily visionaries; rather, they are able to think through plans and initiatives in a way that is consistent with the overall direction of the organization and that takes into consideration risks and contingencies. They analyze what is going on in the current social, political, and organizational environment and determine the impact on their current and future plans.

Why it's important: *Strategic Thinking* allows you to make the right choices to maintain a competitive advantage. It helps you to identify threats and opportunities to the company, the industry, and your career. Instead of focusing on the *how-to* aspects of management, practicing *Strategic Thinking* puts your focus on *what to do* to set a viable long-term direction for yourself, your team, and your organization.

Leading Implementation

This category of skills is all about how you get things done—the execution of the strategy. Those who quickly climb the ranks demonstrate a strong ability to execute. One interesting thing we have noticed is that those with strong creativity, innovation, and vision skills tend to focus less on execution and implementation, and vice versa. Strong leaders are able to excel at both categories of skills.

Coaching and Mentoring

Coaching is the skill of helping other people to solve their own problems and learning through experience so they can function autonomously. Leaders who coach help to shift their team members' mind-sets, change behaviors, improve performance, and take accountability for their own successes. They help people find their own answers. In contrast, leaders who mentor provide others with insights from their own experience on how they can be more effective. Mentors provide the knowledge, wisdom, and direct guidance to assist others in their short- and long-term career goals.

Why it's important: Coaching is critical to success in today's business environment because most of the roles we are assigned require us to face new challenges. Teaching people how to fish (so to speak) increases their competence and decreases their reliance on you. That makes coaching extremely important as your team grows and you take on more responsibility. Meanwhile, mentoring helps others shorten their learning curves for higher levels of productivity by leveraging your experience. The combination of *Coaching and Mentoring* can be very powerful. Tell your story and give your perspective, and then ask how it applies to the other person's situation and what actions he or she can take.

Customer Focus

Customer Focus is about being proactive in ensuring that customers are well served. Customer-focused leaders are clear on who their customers are, work hard to understand their needs and how best to serve them, and solve their problems.

Why it's important: Nothing is more important to a successful organization than its customers. They are the key to an organization's existence and the most valuable source of information to grow and improve the business. They offer the best glimpse into potential new ideas and improvements to existing products or services. When you effectively focus on your customers, they become partners in your success, and you become a partner in their success. This powerful symbiotic relationship is a critical competitive advantage.

Delegation

Delegation is the ability to assign responsibility for certain tasks to others to increase individual and team productivity. Leaders who practice *Delegation* empower others to "own" their project and motivate them to excel at their job. They give others the opportunity to shine.

Why it's important: Delegation is perhaps the most important skill when it comes to your overall productivity and value to the organization as a leader. The more effectively you delegate tasks to others, the more time you will have to strategize and develop new or ongoing initiatives. The more you delegate, the more you can take on, and the higher up you can move.

Effectiveness

Effective leaders get the job done and do it well. They ensure the right people are involved to get the work completed and that key stakeholders are kept informed through proactive communication. They combine their abilities to execute on well-organized plans and create strong morale and spirit in their teams. They bring out the best in each team member in terms of performance and responsibility.

Why it's important: People need to be able to rely on leaders who can get the job done. When you demonstrate *Effectiveness*, you are regarded as a go-to person in your organization, someone who can be counted on to deliver, garner support, and keep the organization's best interests in mind. The more effectively you perform your duties, the more valuable you are to the organization.

Monitoring Performance

Monitoring Performance is the ability to measure and track the performance of staff, projects, and overall objectives. It combines systematically tracking metrics; assessing progress toward identified milestones; holding others accountable; and providing feedback, guidance, and coaching.

Why it's important: Life is full of surprises. The factors that are critical to the success of a project or initiative can quickly change and thus render your plan obsolete. Sometimes people misunderstand their roles or your requests, or they simply don't follow through. Without the tools and processes in place to monitor and manage performance, your effectiveness and ability to lead can be called into question, and you can put yourself at risk of blown budgets, delayed schedules, and outright failure.

Planning and Organizing

Planning and Organizing is a core management skill. Leaders with strong *Planning and Organizing* skills can successfully conceive, develop, and implement plans to accomplish short- and long-term goals. They ensure a thoughtful and systematic course of action in everything from strategic forecasting to allocating resources to everyday scheduling.

Why it's important: Effective *Planning and Organizing* helps you to get things done efficiently and seamlessly. Your team needs to know who is doing what and by when to stay on track. Your role as a leader is to provide that direction by effectively managing your resources and coordinating with other teams, if necessary, to reach milestones and achieve your deliverables.

Thoroughness

Thoroughness necessitates a focused attention to detail without losing sight of the big picture. Thorough leaders prioritize both the end goal and the individual steps they need to take to achieve it. They have an intimate understanding of how each step contributes to the next and are committed to seeing a project to the end.

Why it's important: As a leader, you don't want anything to slip past you. It's important that you be on top of things. Your *Thoroughness* (or lack thereof) can be the difference between a great job, an acceptable job, and something you have to do over. Your future success will be tied to your past *Thoroughness* time and again.

Appendix B
Hidden Strengths Development Worksheet

Step 1: Find Your Motivation

Why are you doing this? By keeping what motivates you up front, you will be more dedicated and disciplined in your efforts to grow and change. The three key sources of professional motivation are security (compensation and benefits, and job security), identity (organizational and self), and stimulation (new and different experiences and gaining mastery in new skill areas). Make sure that the reasons for change are meaningful and sustainable for you.

Step 2: Identify Your Goals

What do you need to accomplish over the next year in order to move up? Make sure these goals are aligned with the larger company vision and strategy. Which categories of skills—Leading Self, Leading Other, Leading the Organization, or Leading Implementation—will you need to use to achieve these goals?

Step 3: Choose Your Hidden Strengths to Develop

Look for patterns in your middle range of skills. Find a cluster of complementary skills that supports your goals over the next year. These are the Hidden Strengths that you should develop next.

Step 4: Turn Your Hidden Strengths into Learned Strengths

Figure out the behaviors you have to change and the new behaviors you need to adopt to turn your Hidden Strengths into Learned Strengths. Talk to your manager and HR department, and do your own research. Make every interaction—meetings, calls, presentations, emails, hallway conversations, and so on—an opportunity to practice these new skills.

Step 5: Evaluate Progress

Ask yourself after every interaction: What did I learn? What should I do differently the next time? Get feedback from others to keep you motivated and on the right track. Be sure to give context, and be specific about what you want to know. These conversations will also help to spread the story of your professional evolution.

Notes

1. Michael M. Lombardo and Robert W. Eichinger, "High Potentials as Learners," *Human Resources* 39, no. 4 (2000): 321–329. http://www.lifetransition.co.uk/pdf/high-poarticle.pdf; Morgan W. McCall, Michael M. Lombardo, and Ann M. Morrison, *The Lessons of Experience: How Successful Executives Develop on the Job* (New York: Free Press, 1998); Ann M. Morrison, Randall P. White, and Ellen Van Velsor, *Breaking the Glass Ceiling: Can Women Reach the Top of America's Largest Corporations?* (New York: Basic Books, 1992).

2. Lombardo and Eichinger, "High Potentials as Learners"; McCall, Lombardo, and Morrison, *Lessons of Experience*; Morrison, White, and Van Velsor, *Breaking the Glass Ceiling*.

3. Marcus Buckingham and Donald O. Clifton, *Now, Discover Your Strengths* (New York: Gallup Press, 2013).

4. Lombardo and Eichinger, "High Potentials as Learners."

5. McCall, Lombardo, and Morrison, *Lessons of Experience*; Morrison, White, and Van Velsor, *Breaking the Glass Ceiling*.

6. Lisa Vollmer, "Anne Mulcahy: The Keys to Turnaround at Xerox," *Insights by Stanford Business*, December 1, 2004. https://www.gsb.stanford.edu/insights/anne-mulcahy-keys-turnaround-xerox

7. K. Anders Ericsson, Ralf Th. Krampe, and Clemens Tesch-Romer, "The Role of Deliberate Practice in the Acquisition of Expert Performance," *Psychological Review* 100, no. 3 (1993): 363–406. http://graphics8.nytimes.com/images/blogs/freakonomics/pdf/DeliberatePractice(PsychologicalReview).pdf

8. Asenath La Rue, "Healthy Brain Aging: Role of Cognitive Reserve, Cognitive Stimulation, and Cognitive Exercises," *Clinics in Geriatric Medicine* 26, no. 1 (2010): 99–111.

9. Barbara Strauch, "How to Train the Aging Brain," *New York Times*, December 29, 2009. http://www.nytimes.com/2010/01/03/education/edlife/03adult-t.html?_r=0

10. Strauch, "How to Train the Aging Brain."

11. Abraham Maslow, "A Theory of Human Motivation," *Psychological Review* 50, no. 4 (1943): 370–396.

12. Allan H. Church, "Managerial Self-Awareness in High-Performing Individuals in Organizations," *Journal of Applied Psychology* 82 (1997): 281–292; Fabio Sala, "Executive Blind Spots: Discrepancies between Self- and Other-Ratings," *Consulting Psychology Journal: Practice & Research* 55 (2003): 222–229.

13. J. Evelyn Orr, Victoria V. Swisher, King Yii Tang, and Kenneth P. De Meuse, "Illuminating Blind Spots and Hidden Strengths," *The Korn/Ferry Institute*, September 2010. http://www.kornferry.com/media/lominger_pdf/Insights_Illuminating_Blind_Spots_and_Hidden_Strengths.pdf

14. Stephen Zaccaro, *The Nature of Executive Leadership: A Conceptual and Empirical Analysis of Success* (Washington, DC: American Psychological Association, 2001).

15. Lombardo and Eichinger, "High Potentials as Learners."

Accessing Your Free
Hidden Strengths Profile

You can create your unique profile at HiddenStrengths.com to get the most from this book and unleash your hidden strengths. You will be asked for the hardcover ISBN (International Standard Book Number) of this book to unlock this valuable tool. The ISBN number can be found at the beginning of the book on the copyright page. (Please use the hardcover ISBN regardless of the format of the book you are reading.) The website will also prompt you to answer some simple verification questions, the answers to which can be found in this book. May you find many new strengths to master!

Acknowledgements

We are fortunate that so many people believed in us and the ideas we wanted to get out into the world. Thus, our thanks go the following people and teams. We thank our book agent, Kimberley Cameron, for believing in the concept. Berrett-Koehler has been the most amazing team of publishing professionals to work with. Everyone we worked with, from sales to distribution to marketing, was top-notch. They made us feel like part of the Berrett-Koehler family. In particular, special thanks go to Jeevan Sivasubramaniam, managing director of the Editorial Department at Berrett-Koehler, for listening to our ideas and immediately seeing the possibilities. We also thank our editors, Neal Maillet and Danielle Goodman, for their guidance in introducing this book to the world. We could not have done it without all of you and your support.

Index

360-degree assessments, 22, 29–30, 54, 57

assertiveness, 15, 34, 51, 52, 54, 60, 68–69
assessments, self. *See* 360-degree
　assessments; Hidden Strengths
　Assessment

Buckingham, Marcus, 9

Clifton, Donald, 9
coaching and mentoring, 38, 50, 51, 54,
　56, 74
conflict resolution, 34, 69
creativity and innovation, 22, 36, 54,
　57, 71
customer focus, 38, 74–75

delegation, 38–39, 51, 54, 56, 57, 75
development plan, 47, 50–51, 59–61,
　63, 77

effectiveness, 13, 38, 56–57, 75
emotional control, 32, 43, 51, 54, 56,
　57, 66
entrepreneurship, 17, 36, 54, 60, 71–72
evaluating progress, 47, 60–63, 77–78
executive presence, 33, 67–68
external awareness, 36–37, 54, 72

flexibility, 17, 32, 54, 56, 57, 66

goals, 49–50, 77

Hidden Strengths Assessment, 10–11, 27,
　30, 41, 47; Barry, CEO, 54–56; George,
　42; Jessica, VP, 56–59; John, 51–54
hidden strengths, value of, 2–3

HiddenStrengths.com, 10, 27, 81

individual contributors, 17
influencing others, 10–11, 22, 23, 34–35,
　43, 57, 69
inspirational vision, 12, 13, 37, 41, 57,
　72–73
integrity, 32–33, 43, 66–67

leadership skills, 17, 41; categories,
　30–31, 43, 50, 67; practice in, 23, 62
leading implementation, 12, 30, 31,
　38–40, 67, 74–76
leading others, 12–13, 30, 31–34, 43, 51,
　67, 68–71
leading self, 30–34, 66–68
leading the organization, 30, 31, 36–38,
　68, 71–74
learned strengths, 11, 17, 23–24,
　62, 77
listening, 14, 35, 50, 54, 57, 59, 61,
　69–70

Maslow's Hierarchy of Needs, 48
Mezirow, Jack, 25
monitoring performance, 39, 75–76
motivation, 47–49, 77
Mulcahy, Anne (Xerox), 21

natural strengths, 2, 7–10, 43, 54, 57
New York Times, 25
Now, Discover Your Strengths, 8

organizational awareness, 15, 37, 73

partnering and relationship building, 13,
　35, 43, 52, 54, 70

planning and organizing, 12–13, 39,
57, 76

resilience, 33, 50, 56, 57, 67

Sales Executive Council, 21–22
self-awareness, 62
self-confidence, 24, 33, 67
self-knowledge, 16
service motivation, 37, 73
skills: adaptation and evolution of, 14;
development of, 19–21, 24–25; middle
set, 22; strengths and weaknesses, 7, 8, 9.
See also leadership skills
stagnation, 3, 14, 16, 22

strategic thinking, 12–13, 37–38, 41, 57,
73–74
strengths, definition of, 8–9

Taylor, Kathleen, 25
teamwork and collaboration, 13,
35, 70
thoroughness, 39, 40, 41, 51, 57, 76
traits and talents for leadership, 19–21

verbal communication, 12–13, 36, 71

weaknesses, dealing with, 2, 11–12, 23,
44, 56
work/life balance, 33, 68

About the Authors

Thuy Sindell is the founder and president of Skyline Group International's Coaching Division. She holds a doctorate in organizational psychology. She is the author of *Sink or Swim* (2006), *Job Spa* (2008), and *The End of Work as You Know It* (2010). Thuy is an executive coach for a number of leaders in Fortune 500 and fast-growing companies. Her passion is to help leaders quickly determine where to best focus their energy for maximum impact on their coworkers, the organization, and the world.

Milo Sindell is also a president at Skyline Group where he oversees the direction, product road map, and market position of the company. He is the author of four books on leadership and employee performance. Milo has been featured in *Business Week*, *CNN*, *Forbes*, *Fortune*, *Investors Business Daily*, *NBC*, and the *Washington Post*.

Berrett–Koehler
Publishers

Connecting people and ideas
to create a world that works for all

Dear Reader,

Thank you for picking up this book and joining our worldwide community of Berrett-Koehler readers. We share ideas that bring positive change into people's lives, organizations, and society.

To welcome you, we'd like to offer you a free e-book. You can pick from among twelve of our bestselling books by entering the promotional code BKP92E here: http://www.bkconnection.com/welcome.

When you claim your free e-book, we'll also send you a copy of our e-newsletter, the *BK Communiqué*. Although you're free to unsubscribe, there are many benefits to sticking around. In every issue of our newsletter you'll find

- A free e-book
- Tips from famous authors
- Discounts on spotlight titles
- Hilarious insider publishing news
- A chance to win a prize for answering a riddle

Best of all, our readers tell us, "Your newsletter is the only one I actually read." So claim your gift today, and please stay in touch!

Sincerely,

Charlotte Ashlock
Steward of the BK Website

Questions? Comments? Contact me at bkcommunity@bkpub.com.

MIX
Paper from
responsible sources
FSC® C002589

Certified

B

Corporation
bcorporation.net